The Duties of Parents and Tho

The Duties of Parents

Train up a child in the way he should go; and when he is old, he will not depart from it." Proverbs 23: 6.

I suppose that most professing Christians are acquainted with the text at the head of this page. The sound of it is probably familiar to your ears, like an old tune. It is likely you have heard it, or read it, talked of it, or quoted it, many a time. Is it not so?

But, after all, how little is the substance of this text regarded! The doctrine it contains appears scarcely known, the duty it puts before us seems fearfully seldom practiced. Reader, do I not speak the truth?

It cannot be said that the subject is a new one. The world is old, and we have the experience of nearly six thousand years to help us. We live in days when there is a mighty zeal for education in every quarter. We hear of new schools rising on all sides. We are told of new systems, and new books for the young, of every sort and description. And still for all this, the vast majority of children are manifestly not trained in the way they should go, for when they grow up to man's estate, they do not walk with God.

Now how shall we account for this state of things? The plain truth is, the Lord's commandment in our text is not regarded; and therefore the Lord's promise in our text is not fulfilled.

Reader, these things may well give rise to great searchings of heart. Suffer then a word of exhortation from a minister, about the right training of children. Believe me, the subject is one that should come home to every conscience, and make every one ask himself the question, "Am I in this matter doing what I can?"

It is a subject that concerns almost all. There is hardly a household that it does not touch. Parents, nurses, teachers, godfathers, godmothers, uncles, aunts, brothers, sisters,—all have an interest in it. Few can be found, I think, who might not influence some parent in the management of his family, or affect the training of some child by suggestion or advice. All of us, I suspect, can do something here, either directly or indirectly, and I wish to stir up all to bear this in remembrance.

It is a subject, too, on which all concerned are in great danger of coming short of their duty. This is preeminently a point in which men can see the faults of their neighbors more clearly than their own. They will often bring up their children in the very path which they have denounced to their friends as unsafe. They will see motes in other men's families, and overlook beams in their own. They will be quick sighted as eagles in detecting mistakes abroad, and yet blind as bats to fatal errors which are daily going on at home. They will be wise about their brother's house, but foolish about their own flesh and blood. Here, if anywhere, we have need to suspect our own judgment. This, too, you will do well to bear in mind.

As a minister, I cannot help remarking that there is hardly any subject about which people seem so tenacious as they are about their children. I have sometimes been perfectly astonished at the slowness of sensible Christian parents to allow that their own children are in fault, or deserve blame. There are not a few people to whom I would far rather speak about their own sins, than tell them their children had done anything wrong.

Come now, and let me place before you a few hints about right training. God the Father, God the Son, God the Holy Spirit bless them, and make them words in season to you all. Reject them not because they are blunt and simple; despise them not because they contain nothing new. Be very sure, if you would train children for heaven, they are hints that ought not to be lightly set aside.

I. First, then, if you would train your children rightly, train them in the way they should go, and not in the way that they would.

Remember children are born with a decided bias towards evil, and therefore if you let them choose for themselves, they are certain to choose wrong.

The mother cannot tell what her tender infant may grow up to be,—tall or short, weak or strong, wise or foolish he may be any of these things or not,—it is all uncertain. But one thing the mother can say with certainty: he will have a corrupt and sinful heart. It is natural to us to do wrong. "Foolishness," says Solomon, "is bound in the heart of a child" (Prov. xxii. 15). "A child left to himself brings his mother to shame" (Prov. xxix. 15). Our hearts are like the earth on which we tread; let it alone, and it is sure to bear weeds.

If, then, you would deal wisely with your child, you must not leave him to the guidance of his own will. Think for him, judge for him, act for him, just as you would for one weak and blind; but for pity's sake, give him not up to his own wayward tastes and inclinations. It must not be his likings and wishes that are consulted. He knows not yet what is good for his mind and soul, any more than what is good for his body. You do not let him decide what he shall eat, and what he shall drink, and how he shall be clothed. Be consistent, and deal with his mind in like manner. Train him in the way that is scriptural and right, and not in the way that he fancies.

If you cannot make up your mind to this first principle of Christian training, it is useless for you to read any further. Self-will is almost the first thing that appears in a child's mind; and it must be your first step to resist it.

II. Train up your child with all tenderness, affection, and patience.

I do not mean that you are to spoil him, but I do mean that you should let him see that you love him.

Love should be the silver thread that runs through all your conduct. Kindness, gentleness, long-suffering, forbearance, patience, sympathy, a willingness to enter into childish troubles, a readiness to take part in childish joys,—these are the cords by which a child may be led most easily,—these are the clues you must follow if you would find the way to his heart.

Few are to be found, even among grown-up people, who are not more easy to draw than to drive. There is that in all our minds which rises in arms against compulsion; we set up our backs and stiffen our necks at the very idea of a forced obedience. We are like young horses in the hand of a breaker: handle them kindly, and make much of them, and by and by you may guide them with thread; use them roughly and violently, and it will be many a month before you get the mastery of them at all.

Now children's minds are cast in much the same mold as our own. Sternness and severity of manner chill them and throw them back. It shuts up their hearts, and you will weary yourself to find the door. But let them only see that you have an affectionate feeling towards them,—that you are really desirous to make them happy, and do them good,—that if you punish them, it is intended for their profit, and that, like the pelican, you would give your heart's blood to nourish their souls; let them see this, I say, and they will soon be all your own. But they must be wooed with kindness, if their attention is ever to be won.

And surely reason itself might teach us this lesson. Children are weak and tender creatures, and, as such, they need patient and considerate treatment. We must handle them delicately, like frail machines, lest by rough fingering we do more harm than good. They are like young plants, and need gentle watering, —often, but little at a time.

We must not expect all things at once. We must remember what children are, and teach them as they are able to bear. Their minds are like a lump of metal— not to be forged and made useful at once, but only by a succession of little blows. Their understandings are like narrow-necked vessels: we must pour in the wine of knowledge gradually, or much of it will be spilled and lost. "Line upon line, and precept upon precept, here a little and there a little," must be our rule. The whetstone does its work slowly, but frequent rubbing will bring the scythe to a fine edge. Truly there is need of patience in training a child, but without it nothing can be done.

Nothing will compensate for the absence of this tenderness and love. A minister may speak the truth as it is in Jesus, clearly, forcibly, unanswerably; but if he does not speak it in love, few souls will be won. Just so you must set before your children their duty,—command, threaten, punish, reason, — but if affection be wanting in your treatment, your labor will be all in vain.

Love is one grand secret of successful training. Anger and harshness may frighten, but they will not persuade the child that you are right; and if he sees you often out of temper, you will soon cease to have his respect. A father who speaks to his son as Saul did to Jonathan (1 Sam. xx. 30), need not expect to retain his influence over that son's mind.

Try hard to keep up a hold on your child's affections. It is a dangerous thing to make your children afraid of you. Anything is almost better than reserve and constraint between your child and yourself; and this will come in with fear. Fear puts an end to openness of manner;— fear leads to concealment;— fear sows the seed of much hypocrisy, and leads to many a lie. There is a mine of truth in the Apostle's words to the Colossians: "Fathers, provoke not your children to anger, lest they be discouraged" (Col. iii. 21). Let not the advice it contains be overlooked.

III. Train your children with an abiding persuasion on your mind that much depends upon you.

Grace is the strongest of all principles. See what a revolution grace effects when it comes into the heart of an old sinner,—how it overturns the strongholds of Satan,—how it casts down mountains, fills up valleys,—makes crooked things straight,—and new creates the whole man. Truly nothing is impossible to grace.

Nature, too, is very strong. See how it struggles against the things of the kingdom of God,—how it fights against every attempt to be more holy,—how it keeps up an unceasing warfare within us to the last hour of life. Nature indeed is strong.

But after nature and grace, undoubtedly, there is nothing more powerful than education. Early habits (if I may so speak) are everything with us, under God. We are made what we are by training. Our character takes the form of that mold into which our first years are cast.'

"He has seen but little of life who does not discern everywhere the effect of education on men's opinions and habits of thinking. The children bring out of the nursery that which displays itself throughout their lives."—Cecil. We depend, in a vast measure, on those who bring us up. We get from them a color, a taste, a bias which cling to us more or less all our lives. We catch the language of our nurses and mothers, and learn to speak it almost insensibly, and unquestionably we catch something of their manners, ways, and mind at the same time. Time only will show, I suspect, how much we all owe to early impressions, and how many things in us may be traced up to seeds sown in the days of our very infancy, by those who were about us. A very learned Englishman, Mr. Locke, has gone so far as to say: "That of all the men we meet with, nine parts out of ten are what they are, good or bad, useful or not, according to their education."

And all this is one of God's merciful arrangements. He gives your children a mind that will receive impressions like moist clay. He gives them a disposition at the starting-point of life to believe what you tell them, and to take for granted what you advise them, and to trust your word rather than a stranger's. He gives you, in short, a golden opportunity of doing them good. See that the opportunity do not be neglected, and thrown away. Once let slip, it is gone forever.

Beware of that miserable delusion into which some have fallen, — that parents can do nothing for their children, that you must leave them alone, wait for grace, and sit still. These people have wishes for their children in Balaam's fashion,—they would like them to die the death of the righteous man, but they do nothing to make them live his life. They desire much, and have nothing. And the devil rejoices to see such reasoning, just as he always does over anything which seems to excuse indolence, or to encourage neglect of means.

I know that you cannot convert your child. I know well that they who are born again are born, not of the will of man, but of God. But I know also that God says expressly, "Train up a child in the way he should go," and that He never laid a command on man which He would not give man grace to perform. And I know, too, that our duty is not to stand still and dispute, but to go forward and obey. It is just in the going forward that God will meet us. The path of obedience is the way in which He gives the blessing. We have only to do as the servants were commanded at the marriage feast in Cana, to fill the water-pots with water, and we may safely leave it to the Lord to turn that water into wine.

IV. Train with this thought continually before your eyes—that the soul of your child is the first thing to be considered.

Precious, no doubt, are these little ones in your eyes; but if you love them, think often of their souls. No interest should weigh with you so much as their eternal interests. No part of them should be so dear to you as that part which will never die. The world, with all its glory, shall pass away; the hills shall melt; the heavens shall be wrapped together as a scroll; the sun shall cease to shine. But the spirit which dwells in those little creatures, whom you love so well, shall outlive them all, and whether in happiness or misery (to speak as a man) will depend on you.

This is the thought that should be uppermost on your mind in all you do for your children. In every step you take about them, in every plan, and scheme, and arrangement that concerns them, do not leave out that mighty question, "How will this affect their souls?"

Soul love is the soul of all love. To pet and pamper and indulge your child, as if this world was all he had to look to, and this life the only season for happiness— to do this is not true love, but cruelty. It is treating him like some beast of the earth, which has but one world to look to, and nothing after death. It is hiding from him that grand truth, which he ought to be made to learn from his very infancy,.—that the chief end of his life is the salvation of his soul.

A true Christian must be no slave to fashion, if he would train his child for heaven. He must not be content to do things merely because they are the custom of the world; to teach them and instruct them in certain ways, merely because it is usual; to allow them to read books of a questionable sort, merely because everybody else reads them; to let them form habits of a doubtful tendency, merely because they are the habits of the day. He must train with an eye to his children's souls. He must not be ashamed to hear his training called singular and strange. What if it is? The time is short,—the fashion of this world passes away. He that has trained his children for heaven, rather than for earth,—for God, rather than for man, —- he is the parent that will be called wise at last.

V. Train your child to a knowledge of the Bible.

You cannot make your children love the Bible, I allow. None but the Holy Spirit can give us a heart to delight in the Word. But you can make your children acquainted with the Bible; and be sure they cannot be acquainted with that blessed book too soon, or too well.

A thorough knowledge of the Bible is the foundation of all clear views of religion. He that is well-grounded in it will not generally be found a waverer, and carried about by every wind of new doctrine. Any system of training which does not make a knowledge of Scripture the first thing is unsafe and unsound.

You have need to be careful on this point just now, for the devil is abroad, and error abounds. Some are to be found among us who give the Church the honor due to Jesus Christ. Some are to be found who make the sacraments saviors and passports to eternal life. And some are to be found in like manner who honor a catechism more than the Bible, or fill the minds of their children with miserable little story-books, instead of the Scripture of truth. But if you love your children, let the simple Bible be everything in the training of their souls; and let all other books go down and take the second place.

Care not so much for their being mighty in the catechism, as for their being mighty in the Scriptures. This is the training, believe me, that God will honor. The Psalmist says of Him, " You have magnified Your Word above all Your name" (Ps. cxxxviii. 2); and I think that He gives an especial blessing to all who try to magnify it among men.

See that your children read the Bible reverently. Train them to look on it, not as the word of men, but as it is in truth, the Word of God, written by the Holy Spirit Himself,—all true, all profitable, and able to make us wise unto salvation, through faith which is in Christ Jesus.

See that they read it regularly. Train them to regard it as their soul's daily food,—as a thing essential to their soul's daily health. I know well you can not make this anything more than a form; but there is no telling the amount of sin which a mere form may indirectly restrain.

See that they read it all. You need not shrink from bringing any doctrine before them. You need not fancy that the leading doctrines of Christianity are things which children cannot understand. Children understand far more of the Bible than we are apt to suppose.

Tell them of sin, its guilt, its consequences, its power, its vileness: you will find they can comprehend something of this.

Tell them of the Lord Jesus Christ, and His work for our salvation,—the atonement, the cross, the blood, the sacrifice, the intercession: you will discover there is something not beyond them in all this.

Tell them of the work of the Holy Spirit in man's heart, how He changes, and renews, and sanctifies, and purifies: you will soon see they can go along with you in some measure in this. In short, I suspect we have no idea how much a little child can take in of the length and breadth of the glorious gospel. They see far more of these things than we suppose.

As to the age when the religious instruction of a child should begin, no general rule can be laid down. The mind seems to open in some children much more quickly than in others. We seldom begin too early. There are wonderful examples on record of what a child can attain to, even at three years old.

Fill their minds with Scripture. Let the Word dwell in them richly. Give them the Bible, the whole Bible, even while they are young.

VI. Train them to a habit of prayer.

Prayer is the very life-breath of true religion. It is one of the first evidences that a man is born again. "Behold," said the Lord of Saul, in the day he sent Ananias to him, "Behold, he prays" (Acts ix. 11). He had begun to pray, and that was proof enough.

Prayer was the distinguishing mark of the Lord's people in the day that there began to be a separation between them and the world. "Then began men to call upon the name of the Lord" (Gen. iv. 26).

Prayer is the peculiarity of all real Christians now. They pray,—for they tell God their needs, their feelings, their desires, their fears; and mean what they say. The nominal Christian may repeat prayers, and good prayers too, but he goes no further.

Prayer is the turning-point in a man's soul. Our ministry is unprofitable, and our labor is vain, until you are brought to your knees. Until then, we have no hope about you.

Prayer is one great secret of spiritual prosperity. When there is much private communion with God, your soul will grow like the grass after rain; when there is little, all will be at a standstill, you will barely keep your soul alive. Show me a growing Christian, a going forward Christian, a strong Christian, a flourishing Christian, and sure am I, he is one that speaks often with his Lord. He asks much, and he has much. He tells Jesus everything, and so he always knows how to act.

Prayer is the mightiest engine God has placed in our hands. It is the best weapon to use in every difficulty, and the surest remedy in every trouble. It is the key that unlocks the treasury of promises, and the hand that draws forth grace and help in time of need. It is the silver trumpet God commands us to sound in all our necessity, and it is the cry He has promised always to attend to, even as a loving mother to the voice of her child.

Prayer is the simplest means that man can use in coming to God. It is within reach of all,—the sick, the aged, the infirm, the paralytic, the blind, the poor, the unlearned, — all can pray. It avails you nothing to plead want of memory, and want of learning, and want of books, and want of scholarship in this matter. So long as you have a tongue to tell your soul's state, you may and ought to pray. Those words, "You have not, because you ask not" (Jas. iv. 2), will be a fearful condemnation to many in the day of judgment.

Parents, if you love your children, do all that lies in your power to train them up to a habit of prayer. Show them how to begin. Tell them what to say. Encourage them to persevere. Remind them if they become careless and slack about it. Let it not be your fault, at any rate, if they never call on the name of the Lord.

This, remember, is the first step in religion which a child is able to take. Long before he can read, you can teach him to kneel by his mother's side, and repeat the simple words of prayer and praise which she puts in his mouth. And as the first steps in any undertaking are always the most important, so is the manner in which your children's prayers are prayed, a point which deserves your closest attention. Few seem to know how much depends on this. You must beware lest they get into a way of saying them in a hasty, careless, and irreverent manner. You must beware of giving up the oversight of this matter to servants and nurses, or of trusting too much to your children doing it when left to themselves. I cannot praise that mother who never looks after this most important part of her child's daily life herself. Surely if there be any habit which your own hand and eye should help in forming, it is the habit of prayer. Believe me, if you never hear your children pray yourself, you are much to blame. You are little wiser than the bird described in Job, "which leaves her eggs in the earth, and warms them in the dust, and forgets that the foot may crush them, or that the wild beast may break them. She is hardened against her young ones, as though they were not hers: her labor is in vain without fear" (Job xxxix. 14-16).

Prayer is, of all habits, the one which we recollect the longest. Many a grey-headed man could tell you how his mother used to make him pray in the days of his childhood. Other things have passed away from his mind perhaps. The church where he was taken to worship, the minister whom he heard preach, the companions who used to play with him,—all these, it may be, have passed from his memory, and left no mark behind. But you will often find it is far different with his first prayers. He will often be able to tell you where he knelt, and what he was taught to say, and even how his mother looked all the while. It will come up as fresh before his mind's eye as if it was but yesterday.

Reader, if you love your children, I charge you, do not let the seed-time of a prayerful habit pass away unimproved. If you train your children to anything, train them, at least, to a habit of prayer.

VII. Train them to habits of diligence, and regularity about public means of grace.

Tell them of the duty and privilege of going to the house of God, and joining in the prayers of the congregation. Tell those who wherever the Lord's people are gathered together, there the Lord Jesus is present in an especial manner, and that those who absent themselves must expect, like the Apostle Thomas, to miss a blessing. Tell them of the importance of hearing the Word preached, and that it is God's ordinance for converting, sanctifying, and building up the souls of men. Tell them how the Apostle Paul enjoins us not "to forsake the assembling of ourselves together, as the manner of some is" (Heb. x. 25); but to exhort one another, to stir one another up to it, and so much the more as we see the day approaching.

I call it a sad sight in a church when nobody comes up to the Lord's table but the elderly people, and the young men and the young women all turn away. But I call it a sadder sight still when no children are to be seen in a church, excepting those who come to the Sunday School, and are obliged to attend. Let none of this guilt lie at your doors. There are many boys and girls in every parish, besides those who come to school, and you who are their parents and friends should see to it that they come with you to church.

Do not allow them to grow up with a habit of making vain excuses for not coming. Give them plainly to understand, that so long as they are under your roof it is the rule of your house for every one in health to honor the Lord's house upon the Lord's day, and that you reckon the Sabbath-breaker to be a murderer of his own soul.

See to it too, if it can be so arranged, that your children go with you to church, and sit near you when they are there. To go to church is one thing, but to behave well at church is quite another. And believe me, there is no security for good behavior like that of having them under your own eye.

The minds of young people are easily drawn aside, and their attention lost, and every possible means should be used to counteract this. I do not like to see them coming to church by themselves,—they often get into bad company by the way, and so learn more evil on the Lord's day than in all the rest of the week. Neither do I like to see what I call "a young people's corner" in a church. They often catch habits of inattention and irreverence there, which it takes years to unlearn, if ever they are unlearned at all. What I like to see is a whole family sitting together, old and young, side by side,—men, women, and children, serving God according to their households.

But there are some who say that it is useless to urge children to attend means of grace, because they cannot understand them.

I would not have you listen to such reasoning. I find no such doctrine in the Old Testament. When Moses goes before Pharaoh (Ex. x. 9), I observe he says, "We will go with our young and with our old, with our sons and with our daughters: for we must hold a feast unto the Lord." When Joshua read the law, I observe, "There was not a word which Joshua read not before all the congregation of Israel, with the women and the little ones, and the strangers that were conversant among them." "Thrice in the year," says Ex. xxxiv. 23, "shall all your men — children appear before the Lord God, the God of Israel." And when I turn to the New Testament, I find children mentioned there as partaking in public acts of religion as well as in the Old. When Paul was leaving the disciples at Tyre for the last time, I find it said (Acts xxi. 5)," They all brought us on our way, with wives and children, until we were out of the city: and we kneeled down on the shore, and prayed."

Samuel, in the days of his childhood, appears to have ministered unto the Lord some time before he really knew Him. "Samuel did not yet know the Lord, neither was the word of the Lord yet revealed unto him" (1 Sam. iii. 7). The Apostles themselves do not seem to have understood all that our Lord said at the time that it was spoken: "These things understood not His disciples at the first: but when Jesus was glorified, then remembered those who these things were written of Him" (John xii 1 6).

Parents, comfort your minds with these examples. Do not be cast down because your children see not the full value of the means of grace now. Only train them up to a habit of regular attendance. Set it before their minds as a high, holy, and solemn duty, and believe me, the day will very likely come when they will bless you for your deed.

VIII. Train them to a habit of faith.

I mean by this, you should train them up to believe what you say. You should try to make them feel confidence in your judgment, and respect your opinions, as better than their own. You should accustom them to think that, when you say a thing is bad for them, it must be bad, and when you say it is good for them, it must be good; that your knowledge, in short, is better than their own, and that they may rely implicitly on your word. Teach them to feel that what they know not now, they will probably know hereafter, and to be satisfied there is a reason and a needs-be for everything you require them to do.

Who indeed can describe the blessedness of a real spirit of faith? Or rather, who can tell the misery that unbelief has brought upon the world? Unbelief made Eve eat the forbidden fruit,—she doubted the truth of God's word: "You shall surely die." Unbelief made the old world reject Noah's warning, and so perish in sin. Unbelief kept Israel in the wilderness,—it was the bar that kept them from entering the promised land. Unbelief made the Jews crucify the Lord of glory,—they believed not the voice of Moses and the prophets, though read to them every day. And unbelief is the reigning sin of man's heart down to this very hour, — unbelief in God's promises, — unbelief in God's threatenings,— unbelief in our own sinfulness, — unbelief in our own danger,—unbelief in everything that runs counter to the pride and worldliness of our evil hearts. Reader, you train your children to little purpose if you do not train them to a habit of implicit faith,—faith in their parents' word, confidence that what their parents say must be right.

I have heard it said by some, that you should require nothing of children which they cannot understand that you should explain and give a reason for everything you desire them to do. I warn you solemnly against such a notion. I tell you plainly, I think it an unsound and rotten principle. No doubt it is absurd to make a mystery of everything you do, and there are many things which it is well to explain to children, in order that they may see that they are reasonable and wise. But to bring them up with the idea that they must take nothing on trust, that they, with their weak and imperfect understandings, must have the " why " and the "wherefore" made clear to them at every step they take,—this is indeed a fearful mistake, and likely to have the worst effect on their minds.

Reason with your child if you are so disposed, at certain times, but never forget to keep him in mind (if you really love him) that he is but a child after all,—that he thinks as a child, he understands as a child, and therefore must not expect to know the reason of everything at once.

Set before him the example of Isaac, in the day when Abraham took him to offer him on Mount Moriah (Gen. xxii.). He asked his father that single question, "Where is the lamb for a burned-offering?" and he got no answer but this, "God will provide Himself a lamb." How, or where, or where, or in what manner, or by what means,—all this Isaac was not told; but the answer was enough. He believed that it would be well, because his father said so, and he was content.

Tell your children, too, that we must all be learners in our beginnings, that there is an alphabet to be mastered in every kind of knowledge,—that the best horse in the world had need once to be broken,—that a day will come when they will see the wisdom of all your training. But in the meantime if you say a thing is right, it must be enough for them,—they must believe you, and be content.

Parents, if any point in training is important, it is this. I charge you by the affection you have to your children, use every means to train them up to a habit of faith.

IX. Train them to a habit of obedience.

This is an object which it is worth any labor to attain. No habit, I suspect, has such an influence over our lives as this. Parents, determine to make your children obey you, though it may cost you much trouble, and cost them many tears. Let there be no questioning, and reasoning, and disputing, and delaying, and answering again. When you give them a command, let them see plainly that you will have it done.

Obedience is the only reality. It is faith visible, faith acting, and faith incarnate. It is the test of real discipleship among the Lord's people. "You are My friends if you do whatever I command you" (John xv. 14). It ought to be the mark of well-trained children, that they do whatever their parents command them. Where, in deed, is the honor which the fifth commandment enjoins, if fathers and mothers are not obeyed cheerfully, willingly, and at once?

Early obedience has all Scripture on its side. It is in Abraham's praise, not merely he will train his family, but "he will command his children, and his household after him" (Gen. xviii. 19). It is said of the Lord Jesus Christ Himself, that when "He was young He was subject to Mary and Joseph" (Luke ii. 51). Observe how implicitly Joseph obeyed the order of his father Jacob (Gen. xxxvii. 13). See how Isaiah speaks of it as an evil thing, when "the child shall behave himself proudly against the ancient" (Isa. iii. 5). Mark how the Apostle Paul names disobedience to parents as one of the bad signs of the latter days (2 Tim. iii. 2). Mark how he singles out this grace of requiring obedience as one that should adorn a Christian minister: "a bishop must be one that rules well his own house, having his children in subjection with all gravity." And again, "Let the deacons rule their children and their own houses well " (1 Tim. iii. 4, 12). And again, an elder must be one "having faithful children, children not accused of riot, or unruly" (Tit. 1. 6).

Parents, do you wish to see your children happy? Take care, then, that you train them to obey when they are spoken to,—to do as they are bid. Believe me, we are not made for entire independence,—we are not fit for it. Even Christ's freemen have a yoke to wear, they "serve the Lord Christ" (Col. iii.

24). Children cannot learn too soon that this is a world in which we are not all intended to rule, and that we are never in our right place until we know how to obey our betters. Teach them to obey while young, or else they will be fretting against God all their lives long, and wear themselves out with the vain idea of being independent of His control.

Reader, this hint is only too much needed. You will see many in this day who allow their children to choose and think for themselves long before they are able, and even make excuses for their disobedience, as if it were a thing not to be blamed. To my eyes, a parent always yielding, and a child always having its own way, are a most painful sight ; — painful, because I see God's appointed order of things inverted and turned upside down;—painful, because I feel sure the consequence to that child's character in the end will be self-will, pride, and self-conceit. You must not wonder that men refuse to obey their Father which is in heaven, if you allow them, when children, to disobey their father who is upon earth.

Parents, if you love your children, let obedience be a motto and a watchword continually before their eyes.

X. Train them to a habit of always speaking the truth.

Truth-speaking is far less common in the world than at first sight we are disposed to think. The whole truth, and nothing but the truth, is a golden rule which many would do well to bear in mind. Lying and prevarication are old sins. The devil was the father of them, — he deceived Eve by a bold lie, and ever since the fall it is a sin against which all the children of Eve have need to be on their guard.

Only think how much falsehood and deceit there is in the world! How much exaggeration! How many additions are made to a simple story! How many things left out, if it does not serve the speaker's interest to tell them! How few there are about us of whom we can say, we put unhesitating trust in their word! Verily the ancient Persians were wise in their generation: it was a leading point with them in educating their children, that they should learn to speak the truth. What an awful proof it is of man's natural sinfulness, that it should be needful to name such a point at all!

Reader, I would have you remark how often God is spoken of in the Old Testament as the God of truth. Truth seems to be especially set before us as a leading feature in the character of Him with whom we have to do. He never swerves from the straight line. He abhors lying and hypocrisy. Try to keep this continually before your children's minds. Press upon them at all times, that less than the truth is a lie; that evasion, excuse-making, and exaggeration are all halfway houses towards what is false, and ought to be avoided. Encourage them in any circumstances to be straightforward, and, whatever it may cost them, to speak the truth.

I press this subject on your attention, not merely for the sake of your children's character in the world,— though I might dwell much on this,—I urge it rather for your own comfort and assistance in all your dealings with them. You will find it a mighty help indeed, to be able always to trust their word. It will go far to prevent that habit of concealment, which so unhappily prevails sometimes among children. Openness and straightforwardness depend much upon a parent's treatment of this matter in the days of our infancy.

XI. Train them to a habit of always redeeming the time.

Idleness is the devil's best friend. It is the surest way to give him an opportunity of doing us harm. An idle mind is like an open door, and if Satan does not enter in himself by it, it is certain he will throw in something to raise bad thoughts in our souls.

No created being was ever meant to be idle. Service and work is the appointed portion of every creature of God. The angels in heaven work,—they are the Lord's ministering servants, ever doing His will. Adam, in Paradise, had work,—he was appointed to dress the garden of Eden, and to keep it. The redeemed saints in glory will have work, "They rest not day and night singing praise and glory to Him who bought them." And man, weak, sinful man, must have something to do, or else his soul will soon get into an unhealthy state. We must have our hands filled, and our minds occupied with something, or else our imaginations will soon ferment and breed mischief.

And what is true of us, is true of our children too. Alas, indeed, for the man that has nothing to do! The Jews thought idleness a positive sin: it was a law of theirs that every man should bring up his son to some useful trade,—and they were right. They knew the heart of man better than some of us appear to do.

Idleness made Sodom what she was. "This was the iniquity of your sister Sodom, pride, fullness of bread, and abundance of idleness was in her" (Ezek. xvi. 49). Idleness had much to do with David's awful sin with the wife of Uriah.—I see in 2 Sam. xi. that Joab went out to war against Ammon, "but David tarried still at Jerusalem." Was not that idle? And then it was that he saw Bathsheba,—and the next step we read of is his tremendous and miserable fall.

Verily, I believe that idleness has led to more sin than almost any other habit that could be named. I suspect it is the mother of many a work of the flesh, — the mother of adultery, fornication, drunkenness, and many other deeds of darkness that I have not time to name. Let your own conscience say whether I do not speak the truth. You were idle, and at once the devil knocked at the door and came in.

And indeed I do not wonder ;—everything in the world around us seems to teach the same lesson. It is the still water which becomes stagnant and impure: the running, moving streams are always clear. If you have steam machinery, you must work it, or it soon gets out of order. If you have a horse, you must exercise him; he is never so well as when he has regular work. If you would have good bodily health yourself, you must take exercise. If you always sit still, your body is sure at length to complain. And just so is it with the soul. The active moving mind is a hard mark for the devil to shoot at. Try to be always full of useful employment, and thus your enemy will find it difficult to get room to sow tares.

Reader, I ask you to set these things before the minds of your children. Teach them the value of time, and try to make them learn the habit of using it well. It pains me to see children idling over what they have in hand, whatever it may be. I love to see them active and industrious, and giving their whole heart to all they do; giving their whole heart to lessons, when they have to learn;—giving their whole heart even to their amusements, when they go to play.

But if you love them well, let idleness be counted a sin in your family.

XII. Train them with a constant fear of over-indulgence.

This is the one point of all on which you have most need to be on your guard. It is natural to be tender and affectionate towards your own flesh and blood, and it is the excess of this very tenderness and affection which you have to fear. Take heed that it does not make you blind to your children's faults, and deaf to all advice about them. Take heed lest it make you overlook bad conduct, rather than have the pain of inflicting punishment and correction. I know well that punishment and correction are disagreeable things. Nothing is more unpleasant than giving pain to those we love, and calling forth their tears. But so long as hearts are what hearts are, it is vain to suppose, as a general rule, that children can ever be brought up without correction.

Spoiling is a very expressive word, and sadly full of meaning. Now it is the shortest way to spoil children to let them have their own way,—to allow them to do wrong and not to punish them for it. Believe me, you must not do it, whatever pain it may cost you unless you wish to ruin your children's souls.

You cannot say that Scripture does not speak expressly on this subject: "He that spares his rod, hates his son; but he that loves him, chastens him betimes" (Prov. xiii. 24). "Chasten your son while there is hope, and let not your soul spare for his crying" (Prov. xix. 18). "Foolishness is bound in the heart of a child: but the rod of correction shall drive it from him" (Prov. xxii. 15). "Withhold not correction from the child, for if you beat him with the rod he shall not die. You shall beat him with the rod, and deliver his soul from hell" (Prov. xxiii. 13, 14). "The rod and reproof give wisdom: but a child left to himself brings his mother to shame." "Correct your son, and he shall give you rest, yes, he shall give delight to your soul" (Prov. xxix. 15, 17).

How strong and forcible are these texts! How melancholy is the fact, that in many Christian families they seem almost unknown! Their children need reproof, but it is hardly ever given; they need correction, but it is hardly ever employed. And yet this book of Proverbs is not obsolete and unfit for Christians. It is given by inspiration of God, and profitable. It is given for our learning, even as the Epistles to the Romans and Ephesians. Surely the believer who brings up his children without attention to its counsel is making himself wise above that which is written, and greatly errs.

Fathers and mothers, I tell you plainly, if you never punish your children when they are in fault, you are doing them a grievous wrong. I warn you, this is the rock on which the saints of God, in every age, have only too frequently made shipwreck. I would sincerely persuade you to be wise in time, and keep clear of it. See it in Eli's case. His sons Hophni and Phineas "made themselves vile, and he restrained them not." He gave them no more than a tame and lukewarm reproof, when he ought to have rebuked them sharply. In one word, he honored his sons above God. And what was the end of these things? He lived to hear of the death of both his sons in battle, and his own grey hairs were brought down with sorrow to the grave (1 Sam. ii. 22- 29, iii. 13).

See, too, the case of David. Who can read without pain the history of his children, and their sins? Amnon's incest,— Absalom's murder and proud rebellion,—-Adonijah's scheming ambition: truly these were grievous wounds for the man after God's own heart to receive from his own house. But was there no fault on his side? I fear there can be no doubt there was. I find a clue to it all in the account of Adonijah in 1 Kings i. 6: "His father had not displeased him at any time in saying, Why have you done so?" There was the foundation of all the mischief. David was an over-indulgent father,—a father who let his children have their own way,—and he reaped according as he had sown.

Parents, I beseech you, for your children's sake, beware of over-indulgence. I call on you to remember, it is your first duty to consult their real interests, and not their fancies and likings;—to train them, not to humour them—to profit, not merely to please.

You must not give way to every wish and caprice of your child's mind, however much you may love him. You must not let him suppose his will is to be everything, and that he has only to desire a thing and it will be done. Do not, I pray you, make your children idols, lest God should take them away, and break your idol, just to convince you of your folly.

Learn to say "No" to your children. Show those who you are able to refuse whatever you think is not fit for them. Show those who you are ready to punish disobedience, and that when you speak of punishment, you are not only ready to threaten, but also to perform. Do not threaten too much. Threatened folks, and threatened faults, live long. Punish seldom, but really and in good earnest,—frequent and slight punishment is a wretched system indeed.

Some parents and nurses have a way of saying, "Naughty child," to a boy or girl on every slight occasion, and often without good cause. It is a very foolish habit. Words of blame should never be used without real reason.

As to the best way of punishing a child, no general rule can be laid down. The characters of children are so exceedingly different, that what would be a severe punishment to one child, would be no punishment at all to another. I only beg to enter my decided protest against the modern notion that no child ought ever to be whipped. Doubtless some parents use bodily correction far too much, and far too violently; but many others, I fear, use it far too little.

Beware of letting small faults pass unnoticed under the idea "it is a little one." There are no little things in training children; all are important. Little weeds need plucking up as much as any. Leave them alone, and they will soon be great.

Reader, if there be any point which deserves your attention, believe me, it is this one. It is one that will give you trouble, I know. But if you do not take trouble with your children when they are young, they will give you trouble when they are old. Choose which you prefer.

XIII. Train them remembering continually how God trains His children.

The Bible tells us that God has an elect people,—a family in this world. All poor sinners who have been convinced of sin, and fled to Jesus for peace, make up that family. All of us who really believe on Christ for salvation are its members.

Now God the Father is ever training the members of this family for their everlasting abode with Him in heaven. He acts as a husbandman pruning his vines, that they may bear more fruit. He knows the character of each of us,—our besetting sins,—our weaknesses,— our peculiar infirmities,—our special needs. He knows our works and where we dwell, who are our companions in life, and what are our trials, what our temptations, and what are our privileges. He knows all these things, and is ever ordering all for our good. He allots to each of us, in His providence, the very things we need, in order to bear the most fruit,—as much of sunshine as we can stand, and as much of rain,—as much of bitter things as we can bear, and as much of sweet. Reader, if you would train your children wisely, mark well how God the Father trains His. He does all things well; the plan which He adopts must be right.

See, then, how many things there are which God withholds from His children. Few could be found, I suspect, among them who have not had desires which He has never been pleased to fulfil. There has often been some one thing they wanted to attain, and yet there has always been some barrier to prevent attainment. It has been just as if God was placing it above our reach, and saying, "This is not good for you; this must not be." Moses desired exceedingly to cross over Jordan, and see the goodly land of promise; but you will remember his desire was never granted.

See, too, how often God leads His people by ways which seem dark and mysterious to our eyes. We cannot see the meaning of all His dealings with us; we cannot see the reasonableness of the path in which our feet are treading. Sometimes so many trials have assailed us,—so many difficulties encompassed us,—that we have not been able to discover the needs-be of it all. It has been just as if our Father was taking us by the hand into a dark place and saying, "Ask no questions, but follow Me." There was a direct road from Egypt to Canaan, yet Israel was not led into it; but round, through the wilderness. And this seemed hard at the time. "The soul of the people," we are told, "was much discouraged because of the way" (Exod. xiii. 17; Num. xxi. 4).

See, also, how often God chastens His people with trial and affliction. He sends them crosses and disappointments; He lays them low with sickness; He strips them of property and friends; He changes them from one position to another; He visits them with things most hard to flesh and blood; and some of us have well-near fainted under the burdens laid upon us. We have felt pressed beyond strength, and have been almost ready to murmur at the hand which chastened us. Paul the Apostle had a thorn in the flesh appointed him, some bitter bodily trial, no doubt, though we know not exactly what it was. But this we know,—he besought the Lord thrice that it might be removed; yet it was not taken away (2 Cor. xii. 8, 9).

Now, reader, notwithstanding all these things, did you ever hear of a single child of God who thought his Father did not treat him wisely? No, I am sure you never did. God's children would always tell you, in the long run, it was a blessed thing they did not have their own way, and that God had done far better for them than they could have done for themselves. Yes! And they could tell you, too, that God's dealings had provided more happiness for them than they ever would have obtained themselves, and that His way, however dark at times, was the way of pleasantness and the path of peace.

I ask you to lay to heart the lesson which God's dealings with His people is meant to teach you. Fear not to withhold from your child anything you think will do him harm, whatever his own wishes may be. This is God's plan.

Hesitate not to lay on him commands, of which he may not at present see the wisdom, and to guide him in ways which may not now seem reasonable to his mind. This is God's plan.

Shrink not from chastising and correcting him whenever you see his soul's health requires it, however painful it may be to your feelings; and remember medicines for the mind must not be rejected because they are bitter. This is God's plan.

And do not be afraid, above all, that such a plan of training will make your child unhappy. I warn you against this delusion. Depend on it, there is no surer road to unhappiness than always having our own way. To have our wills checked and denied is a blessed thing for us; it makes us value enjoyments when they come. To be indulged perpetually is the way to be made selfish; and selfish people and spoiled children, believe me, are seldom happy.

Reader, do not be wiser than God;—train your children as He trains His.

XIV. Train them remembering continually the influence; of your own example.

Instruction, and advice, and commands will profit little, unless they are backed up by the pattern of your own life. Your children will never believe you are in earnest, and really wish them to obey you, so long as your actions contradict your counsel. Archbishop Tillotson made a wise remark when he said, "To give children good instruction, and a bad example, is but beckoning to them with the head to show them the way to heaven, while we take them by the hand and lead them in the way to hell."

We little know the force and power of example. No one of us can live to himself in this world; we are always influencing those around us, in one way or another, either for good or for evil, either for God or for sin.—They see our ways, they mark our conduct, they observe our behavior, and what they see us practice, that they may fairly suppose we think right. And never, I believe, does example tell so powerfully as it does in the case of parents and children.

Fathers and mothers, do not forget that children learn more by the eye than they do by the ear. No school will make such deep marks on character as home. The best of schoolmasters will not imprint on their minds as much as they will pick up at your fireside. Imitation is a far stronger principle with children than memory. What they see has a much stronger effect on their minds than what they are told.

Take care, then, what you do before a child. It is a true proverb, "Who sins before a child, sins double." Strive rather to be a living epistle of Christ, such as your families can read, and that plainly too. Be an example of reverence for the Word of God, reverence in prayer, reverence for means of grace, reverence for the Lord's day.—Be an example in words, in temper, in diligence, in temperance, in faith, in charity, in kindness, in humility. Do not think your children will practice what they do not see you do. You are their model picture, and they will copy what you are. Your reasoning and your lecturing, your wise commands and your good advice; all this they may not understand, but they can understand your life.

Children are very quick observers; very quick in seeing through some kinds of hypocrisy, very quick in finding out what you really think and feel, very quick in adopting all your ways and opinions. You will often find as the father is, so is the son.

Remember the word that the conqueror Caesar always used to his soldiers in a battle. He did not say "Go forward," but "Come." So it must be with you in training your children. They will seldom learn habits which they see you despise, or walk in paths in which you do not walk yourself. He that preaches to his children what he does not practice, is working a work that never goes forward. It is like the fabled web of Penelope of old, who wove all day, and unwove all night. Even so, the parent who tries to train without setting a good example is building with one hand, and pulling down with the other.

XV. Train them, remembering continually the power of sin.

I name this shortly, in order to guard you against unscriptural expectations.

You must not expect to find your children's minds a sheet of pure white paper, and to have no trouble if you only use right means. I warn you plainly you will find no such thing. It is painful to see how much corruption and evil there is in a young child's heart, and how soon it begins to bear fruit. Violent tempers, self-will, pride, envy, sullenness, passion, idleness, selfishness, deceit, cunning, falsehood, hypocrisy, a terrible aptness to learn what is bad, a painful slowness to learn what is good, a readiness to pretend anything in order to gain their own ends,—all these things, or some of them, you must be prepared to see, even in your own flesh and blood. In little ways they will creep out at a very early age; it is almost startling to observe how naturally they seem to spring up. Children require no schooling to learn to sin.

But you must not be discouraged and cast down by what you see. You must not think it a strange and unusual thing, that little hearts can be so full of sin. It is the only portion which our father Adam left us; it is that fallen nature with which we come into the world; it is that inheritance which belongs to us all. Let it rather make you more diligent in using every means which seem most likely, by God's blessing, to counteract the mischief. Let it make you more and more careful, so far as in you lies, to keep your children out of the way of temptation.

Never listen to those who tell you your children are good, and well brought up, and can be trusted. Think rather that their hearts are always inflammable as tinder. At their very best, they only want a spark to set their corruptions alight. Parents are seldom too cautious. Remember the natural depravity of your children, and take care.

XVI. Train them remembering continually the promises of Scripture.

I name this also shortly, in order to guard you against discouragement.

You have a plain promise on your side, "Train up your child in the way he should go, and when he is old he shall not depart from it" (Prov. xxii. 6). Think what it is to have a promise like this. Promises were the only lamp of hope which cheered the hearts of the patriarchs before the Bible was written. Enoch, Noah, Abraham, Isaac, Jacob, Joseph,—all lived on a few promises, and prospered in their souls. Promises are the cordials which in every age have supported and strengthened the believer. He that has got a plain text upon his side need never be cast down. Fathers and mothers, when your hearts are failing, and ready to halt, look at the word of this text, and take comfort.

Think who it is that promises. It is not the word of a man, who may lie or repent; it is the word of the King of kings, who never changes. Has He said a thing, and shall He not do it? Or has He spoken, and shall He not make it good? Neither is anything too hard for Him to perform. The things that are impossible with men are possible with God. Reader, if we get not the benefit of the promise we are dwelling upon, the fault is not in Him, but in ourselves.

Think, too, what the promise contains, before you refuse to take comfort from it. It speaks of a certain time when good training shall especially bear fruit,—"when a child is old." Surely there is comfort in this. You may not see with your own eyes the result of careful training, but you know not what blessed fruits may not spring from it, long after you are dead and gone. It is not God's way to give everything at once. "Afterwards' is the time when He often chooses to work, both in the things of nature and in the things of grace. "Afterward" is the season when affliction bears the peaceable fruit of righteousness (Heb. xii. 11). "Afterward" was the time when the son who refused to work in his father's vineyard repented and went (Matt. xxi. 29). And "afterward" is the time to which parents must look forward if they see not success at once,—you must sow in hope and plant in hope.

Cast your bread upon the waters," says the Spirit, "for you shall find it after many days" (Eccles. xi. 1). Many children, I doubt not, shall rise up in the day of judgment, and bless their parents for good training, who never gave any signs of having profited by it during their parents' lives. Go forward then in faith, and be sure that your labor shall not be altogether thrown away. Three times did Elijah stretch himself upon the widow's child before it revived. Take example from him, and persevere.

XVII. Train them, lastly, with continual prayer for a blessing on all you do.

Without the blessing of the Lord, your best endeavors will do no good. He has the hearts of all men in His hands, and except He touch the hearts of your children by His Spirit, you will weary yourself to no purpose. Water, therefore, the seed you sow on their minds with unceasing prayer. The Lord is far more willing to hear than we to pray; far more ready to give blessings than we to ask them;—but He loves to be entreated for them. And I set this matter of prayer before you, as the top-stone and seal of all you do. I suspect the child of many prayers is seldom cast away.

Look upon your children as Jacob did on his; he tells Esau they are "the children which God has graciously given your servant" (Gen. xxxiii. 5). Look on them as Joseph did on his; he told his father, "They are the sons whom God has given me" (Gen. xlviii. 9). Count them with the Psalmist to be "an heritage and reward from the Lord" (Ps. cxxvii. 3). And then ask the Lord, with a holy boldness, to be gracious and merciful to His own gifts. Mark how Abraham intercedes for Ishmael, because he loved him, "Oh that Ishmael might live before you" (Gen. xvii. 18). See how Manoah speaks to the angel about Samson, "How shall we order the child, and how shall we do unto him?" (Judg. xiii. 12). Observe how tenderly Job cared for his children's souls, "He offered burned-offerings according to the number of them all, for he said, It may be my sons have sinned, and cursed God in their hearts. Thus did Job continually" (Job i. 5). Parents, if you love your children, go and do likewise. You cannot name their names before the mercy-seat too often.

And now, reader, in conclusion, let me once more press upon you the necessity and importance of using every single means in your power, if you would train children for heaven.

I know well that God is a sovereign God, and does all things according to the counsel of His own will. I know that Rehoboam was the son of Solomon, and Manasseh the son of Hezekiah, and that you do not always see godly parents having a godly seed. But I know also that God is a God who works by means, and sure am I, if you make light of such means as I have mentioned, your children are not likely to turn out well.

Fathers and mothers, you may take your children to be baptized, and have them enrolled in the ranks of Christ's Church;—you may get godly sponsors to answer for them, and help you by their prayers;—you may send them to the best of schools, and give them Bibles and Prayer Books, and fill them with head knowledge but if all this time there is no regular training at home, I tell you plainly, I fear it will go hard in the end with your children's souls. Home is the place where habits are formed;—home is the place where the foundations of character are laid;—home gives the bias to our tastes, and likings, and opinions. See then, I pray you, that there be careful training at home. Happy indeed is the man who can say, as Bolton did upon his dying bed, to his children, "I do believe not one of you will dare to meet me before the tribunal of Christ in an unregenerate state."

Fathers and mothers, I charge you solemnly before God and the Lord Jesus Christ, take every pains to train your children in the way they should go. I charge you not merely for the sake of your children's souls; I charge you for the sake of your own future comfort and peace. Truly it is your interest so to do. Truly your own happiness in great measure depends on it. Children have ever been the bow from which the sharpest arrows have pierced man's heart. Children have mixed the bitterest cups that man has ever had to drink. Children have caused the saddest tears that man has ever had to shed. Adam could tell you so; Jacob could tell you so; David could tell you so. There are no sorrows on earth like those which children have brought upon their parents. Oh! take heed, lest your own neglect should lay up misery for you in your old age. Take heed, lest you weep under the ill—treatment of a thankless child, in the days when your eye is dim, and your natural force abated.

If ever you wish your children to be the restorers of your life, and the nourishers of your old age,—if you would have them blessings and not curses—joys and not sorrows—Judahs and not Reubens—Ruths and not Orpahs,—if you would not, like Noah, be ashamed of their deeds, and, like Rebekah, be made weary of your life by them: if this be your wish, remember my advice betimes, train them while young in the right way.

And as for me, I will conclude by putting up my prayer to God for all who read this paper, that you may all be taught of God to feel the value of your own souls. This is one reason why baptism is too often a mere form, and Christian training despised and disregarded. Too often parents feel not for themselves, and so they feel not for their children. They do not realize the tremendous difference between a state of nature and a state of grace, and therefore they are content to let them alone.

Now the Lord teach you all that sin is that abominable thing which God hates. Then, I know you will mourn over the sins of your children, and strive to pluck them out as brands from the fire.

The Lord teach you all how precious Christ is, and what a mighty and complete work He has done for our salvation. Then, I feel confident you will use every means to bring your children to Jesus, that they may live through Him.

The Lord teach you all your need of the Holy Spirit, to renew, sanctify, and quicken your souls. Then, I feel sure you will urge your children to pray for Him without ceasing, and never rest until He has come down into their hearts with power, and made them new creatures.

The Lord grant this, and then I have a good hope that you will indeed train up your children well,—train well for this life, and train well for the life to come; train well for earth, and train well for heaven; train them for God, for Christ, and for eternity.

Thoughts for Young Men

I. REASONS FOR EXHORTING YOUNG MEN

When the Apostle Paul wrote his Epistle to Titus about his responsibility as a minister, he mentioned young men as a group requiring particular attention. After speaking of older men and older women, and young women, he adds this advice, "Encourage the young men to be self-controlled" (Titus 2:6). I am going to follow the Apostle's advice. I propose to offer a few words of friendly exhortation to young men.

I am growing old myself, but there are few things that I can remember so well as were the days of my youth. I have a most distinct recollection of the joys and the sorrows, the hopes and the fears, the temptations and the difficulties, the mistaken judgments and the misplaced affections, the errors and the aspirations, which surround and accompany a young man's life. If I can only say something to keep some young man walking in the right way, and preserve him from faults and sins, which may hurt his prospects both for time and eternity, I shall be very thankful. There are four things which I propose to do:
I. I will mention some general REASONS why young men need exhorting.
II. I will note some special DANGERS which young men need to be warned about.
III. I will give some general COUNSEL which I beg young men to receive.
IV. I will set down some special RULES OF CONDUCT which I strongly advise young men to follow. On each of these four points I have something to say, and I pray to God that what I say may do good to some soul.

I. REASONS FOR EXHORTING YOUNG MEN

What are the general reasons why young men need specific exhortation? I will mention several of them in order.

(1) For one thing, there is the painful fact that there are few young men anywhere who seem to be Christians.

I speak without respect of persons; I say it of all. Rich or poor, gentle or rough, educated or uneducated, in the city or in the country — it makes no difference. I shudder to think how few young men are led by the Spirit, how few are on that narrow road which leads to life, how few are setting their affections on things above, how few are taking up the cross, and following

Christ. I say all this with sorrow, but I believe, in God's sight, that I am saying nothing more than the truth.

Young men, you form a large and most important class in the population of this country; but where, and in what condition, are your souls? Regardless of where we turn for an answer, the report will be one and the same! Let us ask any faithful minister of the gospel, and note what he will tell us. How many unmarried young people can he remember who come to the Lord's Supper? Who are the most backward about the doctrines of salvation, the most irregular about Sunday services, the most difficult to draw to weekly Bible studies and prayer meetings, the most inattentive to whatever is being preached? Which part of his congregation fills him with the most anxiety? Who are the Reubens for whom he has the deepest "searchings of heart"? Who in his flock are the hardest to manage, who require the most frequent warnings and rebukes, who cause him the greatest uneasiness and sorrow, who keep him most constantly in fear for their souls, and seem the most hopeless? Depend on it, his answer will always be, "The Young Men!"

Let us ask the parents in any county throughout this land, and see what they will generally say. Who in their families give them the most pain and trouble? Who need the most watchfulness, and most often provoke and disappoint them? Who are the first to be led away from what is right, and the last to remember cautions and good advice? Who are the most difficult to keep in order and limits? Who most frequently break out into open sin, disgrace the name they bear, make their friends unhappy, embitter the older relatives, and cause them to die with sorrow in their hearts? Depend on it, the answer will generally be, "The Young Men!"

Let us ask the judges and police officers, and note what they will reply. Who goes to the night clubs and bars the most? Who make up street gangs? Who are most often arrested for drunkenness, disturbing the peace, fighting, stealing, assaults, and the like? Who fill the jails, and penitentiaries, and detention homes? Who are the class which requires the most incessant watching and looking after? Depend on it, they will at once point to the same group, they will say, "The Young Men!"

Let us turn to the upper classes, and note the report we will get from them. In one family the sons are always wasting time, health, and money, in the selfish pursuit of pleasure. In another, the sons will follow no profession, and fritter away the most precious years of their life in doing nothing. In another, they take up a profession as a mere form, but pay no attention to its duties. In another, they are always forming wrong connections, gambling, getting into debt, associating with bad companions, keeping their friends in a constant fever of anxiety. Note that rank, and title, and wealth, and education, do not prevent these things! Anxious fathers, and heart-broken mothers, and sorrowing sisters, could tell sad stories about them, if the truth were known. Many a family, with everything this world can give, numbers among its relatives some name that is never named, or only named with regret and shame, some son, some brother, some cousin, some nephew, who will have his own way, and is a grief to all who know him.

There is seldom a rich family which hasn't got some thorn in its side, some blot in its page of happiness, some constant source of pain and anxiety; and often, far too often — the true cause is, "The Young Men!"

What shall we say to these things? These are facts, plain facts, facts which meet us on every side, facts which cannot be denied. How dreadful this is! How dreadful the thought, that every time I meet a young man, I meet one who is in all probability an enemy of God, traveling on the wide road which leads to hell, unfit for heaven! Surely, with such facts before me, will you not wonder that I exhort you, you must allow that there is a good reason.

(2) Death and judgment are waiting for young men, even as it waits for others, and they nearly all seem to forget it.

Young men, it is appointed for you to die; and no matter how strong and healthy you may be now, the day of your death is perhaps very near. I see young people sick as well as the elderly. I bury youthful corpses as well as aged. I read the names of persons no older than yourselves in every graveyard. I learn from books that, excepting infancy and old age, more die between thirteen and twenty-three than at any other period of life. And yet you live as if you were sure that presently you will never die.

Are you thinking you will pay attention to these things tomorrow? Remember the words of Solomon, "Do not boast about tomorrow, for you do not know what a day may bring forth" (Proverbs 27:1). "I will worry about serious things tomorrow," said an unsaved person, to one who warned him of coming danger; but his tomorrow never came. Tomorrow is the devil's day, but today is God's. Satan does not care how spiritual your intentions are, or how holy your resolutions, if only they are determined to be done tomorrow. Oh, give no place to the devil in this matter! All men don't live to be elderly fathers, like Isaac and Jacob. Many children die before their fathers. David had to mourn the death of his two finest sons; Job lost all of his ten children in one day. Your lot may be like one of theirs, and when death comes, it will be vain to talk of tomorrow, you must go at once.

Do you think that you will have a more convenient time to think about these things? So thought Felix and the Athenians to whom Paul preached to; but it never came. The road to hell is paved with such ideas. Better make sure to work while you can. Leave nothing unsettled that is eternal. Run no risk when your soul is at stake. Believe me, the salvation of a soul is no easy matter. Every one needs a "Great salvation," whether young or old; all need to be born again — all need to be washed in Christ's blood — all need to be sanctified by the Spirit. Happy is that man who does not leave these things uncertain, but never rests until he has the witness of the Spirit within him, testifying to him that he is a child of God.

Young men, your time is short. Your days are but a brief shadow, a mist that appears for a little while and then vanishes, a story that is soon told. Your bodies are not made of brass. "Even the young men," says Isaiah, "stumble and fall" (Isaiah 40:30). Your health may be taken from you in a moment: it only needs an accident, a fever, an inflammation, a broken blood-vessel, and the worm would soon feed upon you in the grave. There is but a step between any one of you and death. This night your soul might be required of you. You are fast going the way of all the earth, you will soon be gone. Your life is all uncertainty, your death and judgment are perfectly sure. You too must hear the Archangel's trumpet, and go forth to stand before the great white throne of judgment, you too must obey that summons, which Jerome says was always ringing in his ears: "Get up, you dead, and come to judgment." "Yes, I am coming soon," is the language of the Judge Himself. I cannot, dare not, will not let you alone.

Oh that you would all take to heart the words of the Preacher: "Be happy, young man, while you are young, and let your heart give you joy in the days of your youth. Follow the ways of your heart and whatever your eyes see, but know that for all these things God will bring you to judgment" (Ecclesiastes 11:9) Amazing, that with such a prospect of coming judgment, any man can be careless and unconcerned! Surely none are so crazy as those who are content to live unprepared to die. Surely the unbelief of men is the most amazing thing in the world. The clearest prophecy in the Bible begins with these words, "Who has believed our message?" (Isaiah 53:1). The Lord Jesus said, "When the Son of Man comes, will he find faith on the earth?" (Luke 18:8). Young men, I fear this be the report of many of you in the courts above: "They will not believe." I fear you be hurried out of the world, and awake to find out, too late, that death and judgment are realities. I fear all this, and therefore I exhort you.

(3) What young men will be, in all probability depends on what they are now, and they seem to forget this.

Youth is the planting time of full age, the molding season in the little space of human life, the turning point in the history of man's mind.

By the shoot that springs up we can judge the type of tree that is growing, by the blossoms we judge the kind of fruit, by the spring we judge the type of harvest coming, by the morning we judge the coming day, and by the character of the young man, we may generally judge what he will be when he grows up.

Young men, do not be deceived. Don't think you can, at will, serve lusts and pleasures in your beginning, and then go and serve God with ease at your latter end. Don't think that you can live with Esau, and then die with Jacob. It is a mockery to deal with God and your souls in such a fashion. It is an awful mockery to suppose you can give the flower of your strength to the world and the devil, and then put off the King of kings with the scraps and remains of your hearts, the wreck and remnant of your powers. It is an awful mockery, and you may find to your loss that the thing cannot be done.

I dare say you are planning on a late repentance. You do not know what you are doing. You are planning without God. Repentance and faith are the gifts of God, and they are gifts that He often withholds, when they have been long offered in vain. I grant you true repentance is never too late, but I warn you at the same time, late repentance is seldom true. I grant you, one penitent thief was converted in his last hours, that no man might despair; But I warn you, only one was converted, that no man might presume. I grant you it is written, Jesus is "Able to save completely those who come to God through him" (Hebrews 7:25). But I warn you, it is also written by the same Spirit, "Since you rejected me when I called and no one gave heed when I stretched out my hand, I in turn will laugh at your disaster; I will mock when calamity overtakes you" (Proverbs 1:24, 26).

Believe me, you will find it no easy matter to turn to God whenever you please. It is a true saying of the godly Leighton, "The way of sin is down hill; a man cannot stop when he wants too." Holy desires and serious convictions are not like the servants of the Centurion, ready to come and go at your desire; rather they are like the unicorn in Job, they will not obey your voice, nor attend at your bidding. It was said of the famous general Hannibal of old, when he could have taken the city he warred against, he would not, and in time when he would, he could not. Beware lest the same kind of thing happens to you in the matter of eternal life.

Why do I say all this? I say it because of the force of habit. I say it because experience tells me that people's hearts are seldom changed if they are not changed when young. Seldom indeed are men converted when they are old. Habits have deep roots. Once sin is allowed to settle in your heart, it will not be turned out at your bidding. Custom becomes second nature, and its chains are not easily broken. The prophet has well said, "Can the Ethiopian change his skin, or the leopard its spots? Neither can you do good who are accustomed to doing evil" (Jeremiah 13:23). Habits are like stones rolling down hill — the further they roll, the faster and more ungovernable is their course. Habits, like trees, are strengthened by age. A boy may bend an oak when it is a sapling — a hundred men cannot root it up, when it is a full grown tree. A child can wade over the Thames River at its fountain-head — the largest ship in the world can float in it when it gets near the sea. So it is with habits: the older the stronger — the longer they have held possession, the harder they will be to cast out. They grow with our growth, and strengthen with our strength. Custom is the nurse of sin. Every fresh act of sin lessens fear and remorse, hardens our hearts, blunts the edge of our conscience, and increases our evil inclination.

Young men, you may fancy I am laying too much stress on this point. If you had seen old men, as I have, on the brink of the grave, without any feelings, seared, callous, dead, cold, hard as stone — you would not think so. Believe me, you cannot stand still in your souls. Habits of good or evil are daily strengthening in your hearts. Every day you are either getting nearer to God, or further off. Every year that you continue unrepentant, the wall of division between you and heaven becomes higher and thicker, and the gulf to be crossed deeper and broader. Oh, dread the hardening effect of constant lingering in sin! Now is the accepted time. See that your decision not be put off until the winter of your days. If you do not seek the Lord when young, the strength of habit is such that you will probably never seek Him at all. I fear this, and therefore I exhort you.

(4) The devil uses special diligence to destroy the souls of young men, and they don't seem to know it.

Satan knows very well that you will make up the next generation and therefore he employs every trick to make you his own. I would not have you to be ignorant of his schemes.

You are those on whom he puts his choicest temptations. He spreads his net with the most watchful carefulness, to entangle your hearts. He baits his trap with the sweetest morsels, to get you into his power. He displays his wares before your eyes with his utmost ingenuity, in order to make you buy his sugared poisons, and eat his accursed treats. You are the grand object of his attack. May the Lord rebuke him, and deliver you out of his hands.

Young men, beware of being taken by his snares. He will try to throw dust in your eyes, and prevent you seeing anything in its true colors. He would eagerly make you think that evil is good, and good is evil. He will paint, cover with gold, and dress up sin, in order to make you fall in love with it. He will deform, and misrepresent, and fabricate true Christianity, in order to make you take a dislike to it. He will exalt the pleasures of wickedness — but he will hide from you the sting. He will lift up before your eyes the cross and its painfulness– but he will keep out of sight the eternal crown. He will promise you everything, as he did to Christ, if you will only serve him. He will even help you to wear a form of Christianity, if you will only neglect the power. He will tell you at the beginning of your lives, it is too soon to serve God — he will tell you at the end, it is too late. Oh, do not be deceived!

You don't know the danger you are in from this enemy; and it is this very ignorance which makes me afraid. You are like blind men, walking among holes and pitfalls; you do not see the perils which are around you on every side.

Your enemy is mighty. He is called "The Prince of this world" (John 14:30). He opposed our Lord Jesus Christ all through His ministry. He tempted Adam and Eve to eat the forbidden fruit, and so brought sin and death into the world. He even tempted David, the man after God's own heart, and caused his latter days to be full of sorrow. He even tempted Peter, the chosen Apostle, and made him deny his Lord. Surely his hostility towards man and God is to be despised.

Your enemy is restless. He never sleeps. He is always going around like a roaring lion, seeking whom he may devour. He is always going back and forth in the earth, and walking up and down on it. You may be careless about your souls: but he is not. He wants your soul to make you miserable, like himself, and will have your soul if he can. Surely his hatred towards men and God is to be despised.

And your enemy is cunning. For thousands of years he has been reading one book, and that book is the heart of man. He ought to know it well, and he does know it — all its weakness, all its deceitfulness, all its folly. And he has a storehouse full of temptations, such as are most likely to do the heart of man the most harm. Never will you go to the place where he will not find you. Go into the city — he will be there. Go into the wilderness — he will be there also. Sit among drunkards — and he will be there to help you. Listen to preaching — and he will be there to distract you. Surely such ill-will is to be despised.

Young men, this enemy is working hard for your destruction, however little you may think it. You are the prize for which he is specially contending for. He foresees you must either be the blessings or the curses of your day, and he is trying hard to effect a place in your hearts early in your life, in order that you may help advance his kingdom each day. Well does he understand that to spoil the bud is the surest way to mar the flower.

Oh that your eyes were opened, like those of Elisha's servant Dothan! Oh that you could see what Satan is scheming against your peace! I must warn you — I must exhort you. Whether you will hear or not, I cannot, dare not, leave you alone.

(5) Young men need exhorting because of the sorrow it will save them, to begin serving God now.

Sin is the mother of all sorrow, and no sort of sin appears to give a man so much misery and pain as the sins of his youth. The foolish acts he did — the time he wasted — the mistakes he made — the bad company he kept — the harm he did himself, both body and soul — the chances of happiness he threw away — the openings of usefulness he neglected; all these things that often embitter the conscience of an old man, throw a gloom on the evening of his days, and fill later hours of his life with self-reproach and shame.

Some men could tell you of the untimely loss of health, brought on by youthful sins. Disease racks their limbs with pain, and life is almost a weariness. Their muscular strength is so wasted, that the slightest weight seems a burden. Their eye has become prematurely dim, and their natural energy abated. The sun of their health has gone down while it is yet day, and they mourn to see their flesh and body consumed. Believe me, this is a bitter cup to drink.

Others could give you sad accounts of the consequences of idleness. They threw away the golden opportunity for learning. They would not get wisdom at the time when their minds were most able to receive it, and their memory most ready to retain it. And now it is too late. They don't have the time to sit down and learn. They no longer have the same power, even if they had the time. Lost time can never be redeemed. This too is a bitter cup to drink.

Others could tell you of grievous mistakes in judgment, from which they suffer all their lives. They had to have it their own way. They would not take advice. They formed some connection which has been altogether ruinous to their happiness. They chose a profession for which they were entirely unsuited. And they see it all now. But their eyes are only open when the mistake cannot be retrieved. Oh, this is also a bitter cup to drink!

Young men, young men, I wish you did but know the comfort of a conscience not burdened with a long list of youthful sins. These are the wounds that pierce the deepest. These are the arrows that drink up a man's spirit. This is the iron that enters into the soul. Be merciful to yourselves. Seek the Lord early, and so you will be spared many a bitter tear.

This is the truth that Job seems to have felt. He says, "You write down bitter things against me and make me inherit the sins of my youth" (Job 13:26). So also his friend Zophar, speaking of the wicked, says, "The youthful vigor that fills his bones will lie with him in the dust" (Job 20:11).
David also seems to have felt it. He says to the Lord, "Remember not the sins of my youth and my rebellious ways" (Psalm 25:7).

Beza, the great Swiss Reformer, felt it so strongly, that he named it in his will as a special mercy that he had been called out from the world, by the grace of God, at the age of sixteen.

Go and ask believers now, and I think many will tell you much the same. "Oh that I could live my young days over again!" He will most probably say, "Oh that I had spent the beginning of my life in a better way! Oh that I had not laid the foundation of evil habits so strongly in the springtime of my journey!"

Young men, I want to save you all this sorrow, if I can. Hell itself is truth known too late. Be wise in time. What youth sows, old age must reap. Do not give the most precious season of your life to that which will not comfort you in the latter days of your life. Sow to yourselves rather in righteousness: break up your hard ground, don't sow among thorns.

Sin may be easy for you to do with your hands, or run smoothly off your tongue now, but depend on it, the effects of your sin and you will meet again in time, however little you may like it. Old wounds will often ache and give pain long after they are healed, and only a scar remains: so may you find it with your sins. The footprints of animals have been found on the surface of rocks that were once wet sand, thousands of years after the animal that made them has perished and passed away; so also may it be with your sins.

"Experience," says the proverb, "is a hard school to attend, but fools will learn in no other." I want you all to escape the misery of learning in that school. I want you to avoid the wretchedness that youthful sins are sure to entail. This is the last reason why I exhort you.

II. DANGERS OF YOUNG MEN

There are some special dangers that young men need to be warned against.

(1) One danger to young men is PRIDE.

I know well that all souls are in fearful peril. Old or young, it doesn't matter; all have a race to run, a battle to fight, a heart to humble, a world to overcome, a body to keep under control, a devil to resist; and we may very well say, Who is sufficient for these things? But still every age and condition has its own peculiar snares and temptations, and it is well to know them. He that is forewarned is forearmed. If I can only persuade you to be on your guard against the dangers I am going to name, I am sure I shall do your souls an essential service.

Pride is the oldest sin in the world. Indeed, it was before the world. Satan and his angels fell by pride. They were not satisfied with their first situation and status. Thus pride stocked hell with its first inhabitants.

Pride threw Adam out of paradise. He was not content with the place God assigned him. He tried to raise himself, and fell. Thus sin, sorrow, and death entered in by pride.

Pride sits in all our hearts by nature. We are born proud. Pride makes us rest content with ourselves--think we are good enough as we are--keep us from taking advice--refuse the gospel of Christ--turn every one to his own way. But pride never reigns anywhere so powerfully as in the heart of a young man.

How common is it to see young men with big heads, high-minded, and impatient of any counsel! How often they are rude and uncourteous to all around them, thinking they are not valued and honored as they deserve! How often will they not stop to listen to a hint from an older person! They think that they know everything. They are full of conceit of their own wisdom. They think elderly people, and especially their relatives, are stupid, and dull, and slow. They want no teaching or instruction themselves: they understand all things. It almost makes them angry to be spoken to. Like young horses, they cannot bear the least control. They must be independent and have their own way. They seem to think, like those whom Job mentioned, "You are the people, and wisdom will die with you" (Job 12:2). And all this is pride.

Rehoboam was such a person, who despised the counsel of the old experienced men who stood before his father, and listened to the advice of the young men of his own generation. He lived to reap the consequences of his folly. There are many like him.

The prodigal son in the parable was also such a person, who needed to have his share of the inheritance so he could set himself up in the lifestyle that he desired. He could not submit to live quietly under his father's roof, but would go into a far country, and be his own master. Like the little child that will leave its mother's hand and walk alone, he soon feels the sting for his folly. He became wiser when he had to eat husks with the swine. But there are many like him.

Young men, I beseech you earnestly, beware of pride. Two things are said to be very rare sights in the world--one is a young man that is humble, and the other is an old man that is content. I fear that this is only too true.

Do not be proud of your own abilities, your own strength, your own knowledge, your own appearance, your own cleverness. Do not be proud of yourself, and your endowments of any kind. It all comes from not knowing yourself and the world. The older you grow, and the more you see, the less reason you will find for being proud. Ignorance and inexperience are the pedestal of pride; once the pedestal is removed--pride will soon come down.

Remember how often Scripture sets before us the excellence of a humble spirit. How strongly we are warned "Do not think of yourself more highly than you ought" (Romans 12:3). How plainly we are told, "The man who thinks he knows something does not yet know as he ought to know!" (1 Corinthians 8:2). How strict is the command, "Clothe yourselves with humility" (Colossians 3:12). And again, "Clothe yourselves with humility" (1 Peter 5:5). This is the garment of which many seem not to have so much as a rag.

Think of the great example our Lord Jesus Christ leaves us in this respect. He washed the feet of His disciples, saying, "You should do as I have done for you" (John 13:15). It is written, "Though he was rich, yet for your sakes He became poor" (2 Corinthians 8:9). And again, "He made Himself nothing, taking the very nature of a servant, being made in human likeness. And being found in appearance as a man, He humbled himself" (Philippians 2:7, 8). Surely to be proud is to be more like the devil and fallen Adam, than like Christ.

Think of the wisest man that ever lived--I mean Solomon. See how he speaks of himself as a "little child," as one who "does not know how to carry out his duties" or manage for himself (1 Kings 3:7). That was a very different spirit from his brother Absalom's, who thought himself equal to anything: "If only I were appointed judge in the land! Then everyone who has a complaint or case could come to me and I would see that he gets justice" (2 Samuel 15:4). That was a very different spirit from his brother Adonijah's, who "exalted himself, saying, I will be king" (1 Kings 1:5). Humility was the beginning of Solomon's wisdom. He writes it down as his own experience, "Do you see a man wise in his own eyes? There is more hope for a fool than for him" (Proverbs 26:12).

Young men, take to heart the Scriptures just quoted. Do not be too confident in your own judgment. Stop being so sure that you are always right, and others wrong. Don't trust your own opinion, when you find it contrary to that of older men, and especially to that of your own parents. Age gives experience, and therefore deserves respect. It is a mark of Elihu's wisdom, in the book of Job, that "Elihu had waited before speaking to Job because they were older than he" (Job 32:4). And afterwards he said, "I am young in years, and you are old; that is why I was fearful, not daring to tell you what I know. I thought, 'Age should speak; advanced years should teach wisdom" (Job 32:6-7). Humility and silence are beautiful graces in young people. Never be ashamed of being a learner: Jesus was one at twelve years; when He was found in the temple, He was "sitting among the teachers, listening to them and asking them questions" (Luke 2:46). The wisest men would tell you they are always learners, and are humbled to find after all how little they know. The great Sir Isaac Newton used to say that he felt himself no better than a little child, who had picked up a few precious stones on the shore of the sea of knowledge.

Young men, if you would be wise, if you would be happy, remember the warning I give you--Beware of pride.

(2) Another danger to young men is the LOVE OF PLEASURE.

Youth is the time when our passions are strongest--and like unruly children, cry most loudly for indulgence. Youth is the time when we have generally our most health and strength: death seems far away, and to enjoy ourselves in this life seems to be everything. Youth is the time when most people have few earthly cares or anxieties to take up their attention. And all these things help to make young men think of nothing except pleasure. "I serve lusts and pleasures:" that is the true answer many a young man should give, if asked, "Whose Servant are you?"

Young men, time would not permit me to tell you all the fruits this love of pleasure produces, and all the ways in which it may do you harm. Why should I speak of carousing, partying, drinking, gambling, movie-going, dancing, and the like? There are few to be found who don't know something of these things by bitter experience. And these are only instances. All things that give a feeling of excitement for the time--all things that drown thought, and keep the mind in a constant whirl--all things that please the senses and delight the flesh--these are the sort of things that have mighty power at your time of life, and they owe their power to the love of pleasure. Be on your guard. Do not be like those of whom Paul speaks, "Lovers of pleasure rather than lovers of God" (2 Timothy 3:4).

Remember what I say: if you would cling to earthly pleasures--these are the things which murder souls. There is no surer way to get a seared conscience and a hard heart towards the things of God, than to give way to the desires of the flesh and mind. It seems like nothing at first, but it tells in the long run.

Consider what Peter says: "Abstain from sinful desires, which war against your soul" (1 Peter 2:11). They destroy the soul's peace, break down its strength, lead it into captivity, and make it a slave.

Consider what Paul says: "Put to death, therefore, whatever belongs to your earthly nature: sexual immorality, impurity, lust, evil desires and greed" (Colossians 3:5). "Those who belong to Christ Jesus have crucified the sinful nature with its passions and desires" (Galatians 5:24). Once the body was a perfect home for a soul--now it is all corrupt and disordered, and needs constant watching. It is a burden to the soul--not a helper; a hindrance--not an assistance. It may become a useful servant, but it is always a bad master.

Consider, again, the words of Paul: "Clothe yourselves with the Lord Jesus Christ, and do not think about how to gratify the desires of the sinful nature" (Romans 13:14). "These," says Leighton, "are the words, the very reading of which gave Augustine a great conviction of heart, causing an immoral young man to be turned into a faithful servant of Jesus Christ." Young men, I wish this might be the case with all of you.

Remember, again, if you cling to earthly pleasures, they will all be unsatisfying, empty, and pointless. Like the locusts of the vision in Revelation, they seem to have crowns on their heads: but like the same locusts, you will find they have stings--real stings--in their tails. All that glitters is not gold. All that tastes sweet is not good. All that pleases for a while is not real pleasure.

Go and take your fill of earthly pleasures if you will--you will never find your heart satisfied with them. There will always be a voice within, crying, like the leech in Proverbs 30:15, "Give! Give!" There is an empty place there, which nothing but God can fill. You will find, as Solomon did by experience, that earthly pleasures are but a meaningless show--promising contentment but bringing a dissatisfaction of spirit--gold plated caskets, exquisite to look at on the outside, but full of ashes and corruption within. Be wise in your youth. Write the word "poison" on all earthly pleasures. The most lawful of them must be used in moderation. All of them are soul-destroying if you give them your heart. Pleasure, must first have the guarantee that it is not sinful--then it is to be enjoyed in moderation.

And I will not shrink from warning all young men to remember the seventh commandment; to beware of adultery and sexual immorality, of all impurity of every kind. I fear that we don't very often speak on this part of God's law. But when I see how prophets and Apostles have dealt with this subject, when I observe the open way in which the Reformers of our own Church denounced it, when I see the number of young men who walk in the wicked footsteps of Reuben, and Hophni, and Phinehas, and Amnon, I for one cannot, with a good conscience, hold my peace. The world becomes more wicked because of our failure to teach and preach on this commandment. For my own part, I feel it would be false and unscriptural delicacy, in addressing men, not to speak of that which is preeminently the "young man's sin."

The violation of the seventh commandment is the sin above all others, that, as Hosea says, "takes away the understanding" (Hosea 4:11). It is the sin that leaves deeper scars upon the soul than any other sin that a man can commit. It is a sin that destroys thousands of young men in every age, and has even overthrown a few of the saints of God in the past. Samson and David are fearful proofs. It is the sin that man dares to smile at, and smoothes over using the terms: thrills, love, uncontrollable passions, and natural desires. But it is the sin that the devil rejoices over, for he is the "unclean spirit;" and it is the sin that God abhors, and declares He "will judge" (Hebrews 13:4).

Young men, "Flee from sexual immorality" (1 Corinthians 6:18) if you love life. "Let no one deceive you with empty words, for because of such things God's wrath comes on those who are disobedient" (Ephesians 5:6). Flee from the opportunity of it--from the company of those who might draw you into it--from the places where you might be tempted to do it. Read what our Lord says about it in Matthew 5:28, "I tell you that anyone who looks at a woman lustfully has already committed adultery with her in his heart." Be like the holy servant Job: "I made a covenant with my eyes not to look lustfully at a girl" (Job 31:1). Flee from talking about it. It is one of the things that ought not even be hinted about in conversation. You cannot even touch black grease without getting your hands dirty. Flee from the thoughts of it; resist them, destroy them, pray against them--make any sacrifice rather than give way to them. Imagination is the hotbed where this sin is too often hatched. Guard your thoughts, and there will be little fear about your actions.

Consider the caution I have been giving. If you forget everything else, do not let this be forgotten.

(3) Another danger to young men is THOUGHTLESSNESS.

Not thinking is one simple reason why thousands of souls are thrown away forever into the Lake of Fire. Men will not consider, will not look ahead, will not look around them, will not reflect on the end of their present course, and the sure consequences of their present days, and wake up to find they are damned for a lack of thinking.

Young men, none are in more danger of this than yourselves. You know little of the perils around you, and so you are careless how you walk. You hate the trouble of serious, quiet thinking, and so you make wrong decisions and bring upon yourselves much sorrow. Young Esau had to have his brother's stew and sold his birthright: he never thought how much he would want it in the future. Young Simeon and Levi had to avenge the rape of their sister Dinah, and kill the Shechemites: they never considered how much trouble and anxiety they might bring on their father Jacob and his house. Job seems to have been especially afraid of this thoughtlessness among his children: it is written, that when they had a feast, and the "period of feasting had run its course, Job would send and have them purified. Early in the morning he would sacrifice a burnt offering for each of them, thinking, 'Perhaps my children have sinned and cursed God in their hearts.' This was Job's regular custom" (Job 1:5).

Believe me, this world is not a world in which we can do well without thinking, and least of all do well in the matter of our souls. "Don't think," whispers Satan: he knows that an unconverted heart is like a dishonest businessman's financial records, they will not bear close inspection. "Consider your ways," says the Word of God--stop and think--consider and be wise. The Spanish proverb says it well, "Hurry comes from the devil." Just as men marry in a rush and then are miserable with their mate, so they make mistakes about their souls in a minute, and then suffer for it for years.

Just as a bad servant does wrong, and then says, "I never gave it a thought," so young men run into sin, and then say, "I did not think about it--it did not look like sin." Not look like sin! What would you expect? Sin will not come to you, saying, "I am sin;" it would do little harm if it did. Sin always seems "good, and pleasant, and desirable," at the time of commission. Oh, get wisdom, get discretion! Remember the words of Solomon: "Make level paths for your feet and take only ways that are firm" (Proverbs 4:26).

Some, I dare say, will object that I am asking what is unreasonable; that youth is not the time of life when people ought to be grave and thoughtful. I answer, there is little danger of their being too much so in the present day. Foolish talking and kidding, and joking, and excessive amusement, are only too common. I don't argue the fact that there is a time for all things; but to be always flippant and joking is anything but wise. What does the wisest of men say--"It is better to go to a house of mourning than to go to a house of feasting, for death is the destiny of every man; the living should take this to heart. Sorrow is better than laughter, because a sad face is good for the heart. The heart of the wise is in the house of mourning, but the heart of fools is in the house of pleasure" (Ecclesiastes 7:2-4). Matthew Henry tells a story of a great statesman in Queen Elizabeth's time, who retired from public life in his latter days, and gave himself up to serious thought. His former merry companions came to visit him, and told him that he was becoming somber: "No," he replied, "I am serious; for everyone around me is serious. God is serious in observing us--Christ is serious in interceding for us--the Spirit is serious in striving with us--the truths of God are serious--our spiritual enemies are serious in their endeavors to ruin us--poor lost sinners are serious in hell--and why then should you and I not be serious too?"

Oh, young men, learn to be thoughtful! Learn to consider what you are doing, and where you are going. Make time for calm reflection. Commune with your own heart, and be still. Remember my caution--Do not be lost merely for the lack of thought.

(4) Another danger to young men is CONTEMPT OF CHRISTIANITY.

This also is one of your special dangers. I always observe that none pay so little outward respect to Christianity as young men. None take so little part in our services, when they are present at them--use Bibles so little--sing so little--listen to preaching so little. None are so generally absent at prayer meetings, Bible Studies, and all other weekday helps to the soul. Young men seem to think they do not need these things--they may be good for women and old men, but not for them. They appear ashamed of seeming to care about their souls: one would almost fancy they considered it a disgrace to go to heaven at all. And this is contempt of Christianity--it is the same spirit which made the young people of Bethel mock Elisha--and of this spirit I say to all young men, Beware! If it is worthwhile to be a Christian, it is worthwhile to be in earnest about it.

Contempt of holy things is the straight road to hell. Once a man begins to make a joke of any part of Christianity, then I am never surprised to hear that he has turned out to be an unbeliever.

Young men, have you really made up your minds to this? Have you clearly looked into the fires which are before you, if you persist in despising Christianity? Call to mind the words of David: "The fool says in his heart, 'There is no God'" (Psalm 14:1). The fool, and no one but the fool has said it: but he has never proved it! Remember, if there ever was a book which has been proved true from beginning to end, by every kind of evidence, that book is the Bible. It has defied the attacks of all enemies and faultfinders. "The Word of the Lord is flawless" (Psalm 18:30). It has been tested in every way, and the more it has been tested, the more evidently has it been shown to be the very handiwork of God Himself. What will you believe, if you do not believe the Bible? There is no choice but to believe something ridiculous and absurd. Depend on it, no man is so grossly naive as the man who denies the Bible to be the Word of God; and if it be the Word of God, be careful that you don't despise it.

Men may tell you that there are difficulties in the Bible; things hard to understand. It would not be God's book if there were not. And what if there are? You don't despise medicines because you cannot explain all that your doctor does with them. But whatever men may say, the things needed for salvation are as clear as daylight. Be very sure of this--people never reject the Bible because they cannot understand it. They understand it too well; they understand that it condemns their own behavior; they understand that it witnesses against their own sins, and summons them to judgment. They try to believe it is false and useless, because they don't like to believe it is true. An evil lifestyle must always raise an objection to this book. Men question the truth of Christianity because they hate the practice of it.

Young men, when did God ever fail to keep His word? Never. What He has said, He has always done; and what He has spoken, He has always made good. Did He fail to keep His word at the flood? No. Did He fail with Sodom and Gomorrah? No. Did He fail with unbelieving Jerusalem? No. Has He failed with the Jews up to this very hour? No. He has never failed to fulfill His word. Take care, lest you be found among those who despise God's

Word.

Never laugh at Christianity. Never make a joke of sacred things. Never mock those who are serious and earnest about their souls. The time may come when you will count those happy whom you laughed at--a time when your laughter will be turned into sorrow, and your mockery into seriousness.

(5) Another danger to young men is the FEAR OF MAN'S OPINION.

"The fear of man" will indeed "prove to be a snare" (Proverbs 29:25). It is terrible to observe the power which it has over most minds, and especially over the minds of the young. Few seem to have any opinions of their own, or to think for themselves. Like dead fish, they go with the stream and tide: what others think is right, they think is right; and what others call wrong, they call wrong too. There are not many original thinkers in the world. Most men are like sheep, they follow a leader. If it was the fashion of the day to be Roman Catholics, they would be Roman Catholics, if it was to be Islamic, they would be Islamic. They dread the idea of going against the current of the times. In a word, the opinion of the day becomes their religion, their creed, their Bible, and their God.

The thought, "What will my friends say or think of me?" nips many a good inclination in the bud. The fear of being looked at, laughed at, ridiculed, prevents many a good habit from being taken up. There are Bibles that would be read this very day, if the owners dared. They know they ought to read them, but they are afraid: "What will people say?" There are knees that would be bent in prayer this very night, but the fear of man forbids it: "What would my wife, my brother, my friend, my companion say, if they saw me praying?" Oh, what wretched slavery this is, and yet how common! "I was afraid of the people and so I gave into them," Saul said to Samuel, "and so he violated the Lord's command" (1 Samuel 15:24). "I am afraid of the Jews," said Zedekiah, the graceless king of Judah: and so he disobeyed the advice which Jeremiah gave him (Jeremiah 38:19). Herod was afraid of what his guests would think of him: so he did that which made him "greatly distressed," he beheaded John the Baptist. Pilate feared offending the Jews: so he did that which he knew in his conscience was unjust--he delivered up Jesus to be crucified. If this is not slavery, what is?

Young men, I want you all to be free from this bondage. I want each of you to care nothing about man's opinion, when the path of duty is clear. Believe me, it is a great thing to be able to say "No!" Here was good King Jehoshaphat's weak point--he was too easy and yielding in his dealings with

Ahab, and therefore caused many of his troubles (1 Kings 22:4). Learn to say "No!" Don't let the fear of not seeming good-natured make you unable to do it. When sinners entice you, be able to say decidedly, "I will not give in to them" (Proverbs 1:10).

Consider how unreasonable this fear of man is. How short lived is man's hostility, and how little harm he can do you! "Who are you that you fear mortal men, the sons of men, who are but grass, that you forget the LORD your Maker, who stretched out the heavens and laid the foundations of the earth?" (Isaiah 51:12-13). And how thankless is this fear! No one will really think better of you for it. The world always respects those the most, who act boldly for God. Oh, break these bonds, and cast these chains from you! Never be ashamed of letting men see that you want to go to heaven. Do not think it a disgrace to show that you are a servant of God. Never be afraid of doing what is right.

Remember the words of the Lord Jesus: "Do not be afraid of those who kill the body but cannot kill the soul. Rather, be afraid of the One who can destroy both soul and body in hell" (Matthew 10:28). Try only to please God, and He will soon make others pleased with you. "When a man's ways are pleasing to the Lord, he makes even his enemies live at peace with him" (Proverbs 16:7). Young men, be of good courage. Don't worry what the world says or thinks: you will not always be with the world. Can man save your soul? No. Will man be your judge in the great and dreadful day of judgment? No. Can man give you a good conscience in this life, a good hope in death, a good answer in the morning of resurrection? No! no! no! Man can do nothing of the sort. Then "Do not fear the reproach of men or be terrified by their insults. For the moth will eat them up like a garment; the worm will devour them like wool" (Isaiah 51:7-8). Call to mind the saying of Gardiner: "I fear God, and therefore I have no one else to fear." Go and be like him.

Such are the warnings I give you. Take them to heart. They are worth thinking about. I am greatly mistaken if they are not greatly needed. The Lord grant that they have not been given to you in vain.

III. GENERAL COUNSELS TO YOUNG MEN

In the third place, I wish to give some general counsels to young men.

(1) TRY TO GET A CLEAR VIEW OF THE EVIL OF SIN.

Young men, if you did know what sin is, and what sin has done, you would not think it so strange that I exhort you as I do. You do not see it in its true colors. Your eyes are naturally blind to its guilt and danger, and therefore you cannot understand what makes me so worried about you. Oh, don't let the devil succeed in persuading you that sin is a small matter!

Think for a moment what the Bible says about sin; how it dwells naturally in the heart of every man and woman alive (Ecclesiastes 7:20; Romans 3:23), how it defiles our thoughts, words, and actions, and that continually (Genesis 6:5; Matthew 15:19), how it renders us all guilty and abominable in the sight of a holy God (Isaiah 64:6; Habakkuk 1:13), how it leaves us utterly without hope of salvation, if we look to ourselves (Psalm 143:2; Romans 3:20), how its fruit in this world is shame, and its wages in the world to come--death (Romans 6:21, 23). Think calmly about all this. I tell you this day, it is just as sad to be dying of cancer and not knowing it, as it is to be a living man, and not know it.

Think what an awful change sin has worked on all our natures. Man is no longer what he was when God formed him out of the dust of the ground. He came out of God's hand upright and sinless (Ecclesiastes 7:29). In the day of his creation he was, like everything else, "very good" (Genesis 1:31). And what is man now? A fallen creature, a ruin, a being that shows the marks of corruption all over, his heart like Nebuchadnezzar, degraded and earthly, looking down and not up, his affections like a household in disorder, calling no man master, all extravagance and confusion, his understanding like a lamp flickering in the socket, impotent to guide him, not knowing good from evil, his will like a rudderless ship, tossed to and fro by every desire, and constant only in choosing any way rather than God's. What a wreck man is, compared to what he might have been! We may understand such figures being used as blindness, deafness, disease, sleep, death, when the Spirit has to give us a picture of man as he is. And man as he is, remember, was made so by sin.

Think, too, what it has cost to make atonement for sin, and to provide a pardon and forgiveness for sinners. God's own Son must come into the world, and take upon Him our nature, in order to pay the price of our redemption, and deliver us from the curse of a broken law. He who was in the beginning with the Father, and by whom all things were made, must suffer for sin the just for the unjust--must die the death of a criminal, before the way to heaven can be laid open to any soul. See the Lord Jesus Christ despised and rejected of men, scourged, mocked, and insulted--look at Him bleeding on the cross of Calvary--hear Him crying in agony, "My God, my God, why have you forsaken me?" Note how the sun was darkened, and the rocks shook at the sight; and then consider, young men, what must be the evil and guilt of sin.

Think, also, what sin has already done on the earth. Think how it threw Adam and Eve out of Eden, brought the flood upon the old world, caused fire to come down on Sodom and Gomorrah, drowned Pharaoh and his army in the Red Sea, destroyed the seven wicked nations of Canaan, scattered the twelve tribes of Israel over the face of the earth. Sin alone did all this.

Think, moreover, of all the misery and sorrow that sin has caused, and is causing, to this very day. Pain, disease, death, strifes, quarrels, divisions, envy, jealousy, malice, deceit, fraud, and cheating, violence, oppression, robbery, selfishness, unkindness, and ingratitude; all these are the fruits of sin. Sin is the parent of them all. It is sin that has so marred and spoiled the face of God's creation.

Young men, consider these things, and you will not wonder that we preach as we do. Surely, if you did think of them, you would break with sin forever. Will you play with poison? Will you sport with hell? Will you take fire in your hand? Will you harbor your deadliest enemy in your arms? Will you go on living as if it mattered nothing, whether your sins were forgiven or not, whether sin had dominion over you, or you over sin? Oh, awake to a sense of sin's sinfulness and danger! Remember the words of Solomon: "Fools mock at making amends for sin, but goodwill is found among the upright" (Proverbs 14:9).

Hear, then, the request that I make of you this day, pray that God would teach you the real evil of sin. If you would have your soul saved then get up and pray.

(2) SEEK TO BECOME ACQUAINTED WITH OUR LORD JESUS CHRIST.

This is, indeed, the principal thing in Christianity. This is the cornerstone of Christianity. Till you know this, my warnings and advice will be useless, and your endeavors, whatever they may be, will be in vain. A watch that does not keep time is as useless as religion without Christ.

But don't let me be misunderstood. It is not the mere knowing of Christ's name that I mean, it is the knowing of His mercy, grace, and power, the knowing of Him not by the hearing of the ear, but by the experience of your hearts. I want you to know Him by faith, I want you, as Paul says, to know "the power of his resurrection; becoming like Him in His death" (Philippians 3:10). I want you to be able to say of Him, He is my peace and my strength, my life and my consolation, my Physician and my Shepherd, my Savior and my God.

Why do I make such a point of this? I do it because in Christ alone "all His [God's] fullness dwells" (Colossians 1:19), because in Him alone there is a full supply of all that we require for the needs of our souls. Of ourselves we are all poor, empty creatures, empty of righteousness and peace, empty of strength and comfort, empty of courage and patience, empty of power to stand, or go on, or make progress in this evil world. It is in Christ alone that all these things are to be found--grace, peace, wisdom, righteousness, sanctification, and redemption. It is just in proportion as we live upon Him, that we are strong Christians. It is only when self is nothing and Christ is all our confidence, it is only then that we shall do great exploits. Only then are we armed for the battle of life, and shall overcome. Only then are we prepared for the journey of life, and shall move forward. To live on Christ, to draw all from Christ, to do all in the strength of Christ, to be ever looking to Christ; this is the true secret of spiritual prosperity. "I can do everything," says Paul, "through Him who gives me strength" (Philippians 4:13).

Young men, I set before you Jesus Christ this day, as the treasury of your souls; and I invite you to begin by going to Him. Let this be your first step-- go to Christ. Do you want to consult friends? He is the best friend: "a friend who sticks closer than a brother" (Proverbs 18:24). Do you feel unworthy because of your sins? Do not fear: His blood cleanses from all sin. He says, "Though your sins are like scarlet, they shall be as white as snow; though they are red as crimson, they shall be like wool" (Isaiah 1:18). Do you feel weak, and unable to follow Him? Do not fear: He will give you the power to become sons of God. He will give you the Holy Spirit to live in you, and seal you for His own; He will give you a new heart, and He will put a new spirit within you. Are you troubled or beset with a strange bent to evil? Do not fear: there is no evil spirit that Jesus cannot cast out, there is no disease of soul that He cannot heal. Do you feel doubts and fears? Throw them aside:

"Come to Me," He says; "whoever comes to me I will never drive away." He knows very well the heart of a young man. He knows your trials and your temptations, your difficulties and your foes. In the days of His flesh He was like yours--a young man at Nazareth. He knows by experience a young man's mind. He can understand the feeling of your temptations--because He Himself suffered when He was tempted. Surely you will be without excuse if you turn away from such a Savior and Friend as this.

Hear the request I make of you this day--if you love life, seek to become acquainted with Jesus Christ.

(3) NEVER FORGET THAT NOTHING IS SO IMPORTANT AS YOUR SOUL.

Your soul is eternal. It will live forever. The world and all that it contains will pass away--firm, solid, beautiful, well-ordered as it is, the world will come to an end. "The heavens will disappear with a roar; the elements will be destroyed by fire, and the earth and everything in it will be laid bare" (2 Peter 3:10). The works of statesmen, writers, painters, architects, are all short lived: your soul will outlive them all. The angel's voice shall proclaim one day, that "There will be no more delay!" (Revelation 10:6). Try, I beg you, to realize the fact, that your soul is the one thing worth living for. It is the part of you which ought always be considered first. No place, no employment is good for you, which injures your soul. No friend, no companion deserves your confidence, who makes light of your soul's concerns. The man who hurts you, your property, your character, only does you temporary harm. Your true enemy is the one who plots to damage your soul.

Think for a moment why you were born into the world. Not merely to eat and drink, and indulge the desires of the flesh, not merely to dress up your body, and follow its lusts wherever they may lead you, not merely to work, and sleep, and laugh, and talk, and enjoy yourselves, and think of nothing but time. No! you were meant for something higher and better than this. You were placed here to train for eternity. Your body was only intended to be a house for your immortal spirit. It is flying in the face of God's purposes to do as many do--to make the soul a servant to the body, and not the body a servant to the soul.

Young men, God does not show favoritism or respects the honors bestowed by men. He rewards no man's heritage, or wealth, or rank, or position. He does not see with man's eyes. The poorest saint that ever died in a ghetto is nobler in His sight than the richest sinner that ever died in a palace. God does not look at riches, titles, education, beauty, or anything of the kind. There is only one thing that God does look at, and that is the immortal soul. He measures all men by one standard, one measure, one test, one criterion, and that is the state of their souls.

Do not forget this. Keep it in view, morning, noon, and night, the interests of your soul. Rise up each day desiring that your soul may excel, lie down each evening, inquiring of yourself whether you soul has really grown. Remember Zeuxis, the great painter of old. When men asked him why he labored so intensely, and took such extreme pains with every picture, his simple answer was, "I paint for eternity." Do not be ashamed to be like him. Set your immortal soul before your mind's eye, and when men ask you why you live as you do, answer them in his spirit, "I live for my soul." Believe me, the day is fast coming when the soul will be the one thing men will think of, and the only question of importance will be this, "Is my soul lost or saved?"

(4) REMEMBER IT IS POSSIBLE TO BE A YOUNG MAN AND YET TO SERVE GOD.

I fear the snares that Satan lays for you on this point. I fear that he will succeed in filling your minds with the vain notion, that to be a true Christian as a youth is impossible. I have seen many carried away by this delusion. I have heard it said, "You are requiring an impossibility in expecting so much Christianity from young people. Youth is no time for seriousness. Our desires are strong, and it was never intended that we should keep them under such strong Christian control, as you wish us to do. God meant for us to enjoy ourselves. There will be plenty of time for religion in the future." And this kind of talk is only too much encouraged by the world. The world is only too ready to wink at youthful sins. The world appears to think it a matter of course that young men must "sow their wild oats." The world seems to take it for granted that young people must be irreligious, and that it is not possible for them to follow Christ.

Young men, I will ask you this simple question--Where will you find anything of this in the Word of God? Where is the chapter or verse in the Bible which will support this talking and reasoning of the world? Doesn't the Bible speak to old and young alike, without distinction? Is not sin--sin, whether committed at the age of twenty or fifty? Will it form the slightest excuse, in the day of judgment, to say, "I know I sinned, but I was young then?" Show your common sense, I beg of you, by giving up such vain excuses. You are responsible and accountable to God from the very moment that you know right and wrong.

I know very well that there are many difficulties in a man's way. But there are always difficulties in the way of doing right. The path to heaven is always narrow, whether we be young or old. There are difficulties, but God will give you the grace to overcome them. God is no hard master. He will not, like Pharaoh, require you to make bricks without straw. He will make sure that the path He requires us to walk is never an impossible road. He never gave commands to man which He would not give man the power to perform.

There are difficulties, but many a young man has overcome them in the past, and so can you. Moses was a young man with passions like yourself; but see what is said of him in Scripture: "By faith Moses, when he had grown up, refused to be known as the son of Pharaoh's daughter. He chose to be mistreated along with the people of God rather than to enjoy the pleasures of sin for a short time. He regarded disgrace for the sake of Christ as of greater value than the treasures of Egypt, because he was looking ahead to his reward" (Hebrews 11:24-26). Daniel was a young man when he began to serve God in Babylon. He was surrounded by temptations of every kind. He had few people with him, and many against him. Yet Daniel's life was so blameless and consistent, that even his enemies could not find any fault in him, except "it has something to do with the law of his God" (Daniel 6:5). And these are not solitary cases. There is a cloud of witnesses whom I could name. Time would not allow me, if I were to tell you of young Isaac, young Joseph, young Joshua, young Samuel, young David, young Solomon, young Abijah, young Obadiah, young Josiah, young Timothy. These were not angels, but men, with natural hearts like your own. They too had obstacles to contend with, lusts to mortify, trials to endure, hard places to travel, like any of you. But young as they were, they all found it possible to serve God. Will they not all rise in judgment and condemn you, if you persist in saying it cannot be done?

Young men, try to serve God. Resist the devil when he whispers it is impossible. Try, and the Lord God of the promises will give you strength in the trying. He loves to meet those who struggle to come to Him, and He will meet you and give you the power that you feel you need. Be like the man whom Bunyan's Pilgrim saw in the Interpreter's house, go forward boldly, saying "Write down my name." Those words of our Lord are true, though I often hear them repeated by heartless and unfeeling tongues: "Seek and you will find; knock and the door will be opened to you" (Matthew 7:7).

Difficulties which seemed like mountains shall melt away like snow in spring. Obstacles which seemed like giants in the distance, will dwindle into nothing when you actually face them. The lion that blocks the way that you are traveling and causes you great fear, will prove to be chained and unable to harm you. If men believed the promises more, they would never be afraid of their assigned duties. But remember that little word I press upon you, and when Satan says, "You cannot be a Christian while you are young:" answer him, "Get behind me, Satan: by God's help I will try."

(5) DETERMINE AS LONG AS YOU LIVE TO MAKE THE BIBLE YOUR GUIDE AND ADVISER.

The Bible is God's merciful provision for sinful man's soul, the map by which he must steer his course, if he would attain eternal life. All that we need to know, in order to make us peaceful, holy, or happy, is richly contained there. If a young man wants to know how to begin his life well, let him hear what David says: "How can a young man keep his way pure? By living according to your word" (Psalm 119:9).

Young men, I charge you to make a habit of reading the Bible, and not to let the habit be broken. Do not Let the laughter of friends, do not let the bad customs of the family you live in, don't let any of these things prevent your doing it. Determine that you will not only have a Bible, but also make time to read it too. Allow no man to persuade you that it is only a book for Sunday school children and old women. It is the book from which King David got wisdom and understanding. It is the book which young Timothy knew from his childhood. Never be ashamed of reading it. Do not "scorn instruction" (Proverbs 13:13).

Read it with the prayer that the Holy Spirit's grace will help you understand it. It has been said, "A man may just as soon read the Scripture without eyes, as understand the spirit of it without grace."

Read it reverently, as the Word of God, not of man, believing implicitly that what it approves is right, and what it condemns is wrong. Be very sure that every doctrine which will not stand the test of Scripture is false. This will keep you from being tossed to and fro, and carried about by the dangerous opinions of these latter days. Be very sure that every practice in your life which is contrary to Scripture, is sinful and must be given up. This will settle many a question of conscience, and cut the knot of many a doubt. Remember how differently two kings of Judah read the Word of God: Jehoiakim read it, and at once tore the page to pieces, and burned it in the fire (Jeremiah 36:23). And why? Because his heart rebelled against it, and he was resolved not to obey. Josiah read it, and at once tore his clothes, and cried mightily to the

Lord (2 Chronicles 34:19). And why? Because his heart was tender and obedient. He was ready to do anything which Scripture showed him was his duty. Oh that you may follow the last of these two, and not the first!

And read it regularly. This is the only way to become "mighty in the Scriptures." A quick glance at the Bible now and then does little good. At that rate you will never become familiar with its treasures, or feel the sword of the Spirit fitted to your hand in the hour of conflict. But store up your mind with Scripture, by diligent reading, and you will soon discover its value and power. Texts will rise up in your hearts in the moment of temptation. Commands will suggest themselves in times of doubt. Promises will come across your thoughts in the time of discouragement. And thus you will experience the truth of David's words, "I have hidden your word in my heart that I might not sin against you" (Psalm 119:11); and of Solomon's words, "When you walk, they will guide you; when you sleep, they will watch over you; when you awake, they will speak to you" (Proverbs 6:22).

I dwell on these things more because this is an age of reading. There seems no end to the producing of many books, though few of them are really profitable. There seems a rage for cheap printing and publishing. Newspapers of every sort abound, and the tone of some, which have the widest circulation, speaks badly for the taste of the age. Amid the flood of dangerous reading, I plead for my Master's book, I call upon you not to forget the book of the soul. Do not let newspapers, novels, and romances be read, while the prophets and Apostles be despised. Do not let the exciting and sensual swallow up your attention, while the edifying and the sanctifying can find no place in your mind.

Young men, give the Bible the honor due to it every day you live. Whatever you read, read that first. And beware of bad books: there are plenty in this day. Take heed what you read. I suspect there is more harm done to souls in this way than most people have an idea is possible. Value all books in proportion as they are agreeable to Scripture. Those that are nearest to it are the best, and those that are farthest from it, and most contrary to it, the worst. (6) Never make an intimate friend of anyone who is not a friend of God.

Understand me, I do not speak of acquaintances. I do not mean that you ought to have nothing to do with anyone but true Christians. To take such a line is neither possible nor desirable in this world. Christianity requires no man to be discourteous.

But I do advise you to be very careful in your choice of friends. Do not open all your heart to a man merely because he is clever, agreeable, good-natured, and kind. These things are all very well in their way, but they are not everything. Never be satisfied with the friendship of any one who will not be useful to your soul.

Believe me, the importance of this advice cannot be overrated. There is no telling the harm that is done by associating with godless companions and friends. The devil has few better helps in ruining a man's soul. Grant him this help, and he cares little for all the armor with which you may be armed against him. Good education, early habits of morality, sermons, books, all, he knows well, will avail you little, if you will only cling to ungodly friends. You may resist many open temptations, refuse many plain snares; but once you take up a bad companion, and he is content. That awful chapter which describes Amnon's wicked conduct about Tamar, almost begins with these words, "Now Amnon had a friend, a very shrewd man" (2 Samuel 13:3).

You must remember, we are all creatures of imitation: precept may teach us, but it is example that draws us. There is that in us all, that we are always disposed to catch the ways of those with whom we live; and the more we like them, the stronger does the disposition grow. Without our being aware of it, they influence our tastes and opinions; we gradually give up what they dislike, and take up what they like, in order to become closer friends with them. And, worst of all, we catch their ways in things that are wrong far quicker than in things that are right. Health, unhappily, is not contagious, but disease is. It is far more easy to catch a chill than to impart a warmth; and to make each other's religion dwindle away, than grow and prosper.

Young men, I ask you to take these things to heart. Before you let any one become your constant companion, before you get into the habit of telling him everything, and going to him with all your troubles and all your pleasures-- before you do this, just think of what I have been saying; ask yourself, "Will this be a useful friendship to me or not?"

"Bad company" does indeed "corrupt good character" (1 Corinthians 15:33). I wish that text were written in the hearts of all young men. Good friends are among our greatest blessings; they may keep us away from much evil, remind us of our course, speak an appropriate word at the right time, draw us upward, and draw us on. But a bad friend is a burden, a weight continually dragging, us down, and chaining us to earth. Keep company with an unsaved man, and it is more than probable you will in the end become like him. that is the general consequence of all such friendships. The good go down to the bad, and the bad do not come up to the good. The world's proverb is only too correct: "Clothes and company tell true tales about character." "Show me who a man lives with and I will show you what he is."

I dwell upon this point, because it has more to do with your prospects in life than first appears. If you ever marry, it is more than probable you will choose a wife from among your circle of friends or their acquaintances. If Jehoshaphat's son Jehoram had not formed a friendship with Ahab's family, he would most likely not have married Ahab's daughter. And who can estimate the importance of a right choice in marriage? It is a step which, according, to the old saying, "either makes a man or ruins him." Your happiness in both lives may depend on it. Your wife must either help your soul or harm it. She will either fan the flame of Christianity in your heart, or throw cold water upon it, and make it burn low. She will either be, wings or handcuffs, an encouragement or an hindrance to your Christianity, according to her character. He that finds a good wife does indeed "finds a good thing;" so if you have the desire to find one, be very careful how you choose your friends.

Do you ask me what kind of friends you should choose? Choose friends who will benefit your soul, friends whom you can really respect, friends whom you would like to have near you on your deathbed, friends who love the Bible, and are not afraid to speak to you about it, friends that you would not be ashamed of having at the coming of Christ, and the day of judgment. Follow the example that David sets for you: he says, "I am a friend to all who fear you, to all who follow your precepts" (Psalm 119:63). Remember the words of Solomon: "He who walks with the wise grows wise, but a companion of fools suffers harm" (Proverbs 13:20). But depend on it, bad company in this life, is the sure way to procure worse company in the life to come.

IV. SPECIAL RULES FOR YOUNG MEN

In the last place, I will set down some particular rules of conduct which I strongly advise all young men to follow.

(1) RESOLVE AT ONCE, BY GOD'S HELP, TO BREAK OFF EVERY KNOWN SIN, HOWEVER SMALL.

Look within, each one of you. Examine your own hearts. Do you see there any habit or custom which you know is wrong in the sight of God? If you do, don't delay for a moment in attacking it. Resolve at once to lay it aside. Nothing, darkens the eyes of the mind so much, and deadens the conscience so surely, as an allowed sin. It may be a little one, but it is not any less dangerous. A small leak will sink a great ship, and a small spark will kindle a great fire, and a little allowed sin in like manner will ruin an immortal soul. Take my advice, and never spare a little sin. Israel was commanded to kill every Canaanite, both great and small. Act on the same principle, and show no mercy to little sins. Well says the book of the Song of Songs, "Catch for us the foxes, the little foxes that ruin the vineyards" (Song of Songs 2:15).

You can be sure that no wicked man ever meant to be so wicked at his first beginnings. But he began with allowing himself some little sins, and that led on to something greater, and that in time produced something greater still, and thus he became the miserable being that he now is. When Hazael heard from Elisha of the horrible acts that he would one day do, he said with astonishment, "How could your servant, a mere dog, accomplish such a feat?" (2 Kings 8:13). But he allowed sin to take root in his heart, and in the end he did them all.

Young men, resist sin in its beginnings. They may look small and insignificant, but mind what I say, resist them, make no compromise, let no sin lodge quietly and undisturbed in your heart. There is nothing finer than the point of a needle, but when it has made a hole, it draws all the thread after it. Remember the Apostle's words, "A little yeast works through the whole batch of dough" (1 Corinthians 5:6).

Many a young man could tell you with sorrow and shame, that he traces the ruin of all his worldly prospects to the point I speak of--to giving way to sin in its beginnings. He began habits of deception and dishonesty in little things, and they grew on him. Step by step, he has gone on from bad to worse, till he has done things that at one time he would have thought impossible till at last he has lost his standing, lost his character, lost his peace, and almost lost his soul. He allowed a gap in the wall of his conscience, because it seemed a little one, and once allowed, that gap grew larger every day, till in time the whole wall seemed to come down.

Remember this especially in matters of truth and honesty. Be careful in even the least syllable spoken. "Whoever can be trusted with very little can also be trusted with much" (Luke 16:10). Whatever the world may like to think, there are no little sins. All great buildings are made up of little parts--the first stone is as important as any other. All habits are formed by a succession of little acts, and the first little act is of mighty consequence. The axe in the fable only begged the trees to let him have one little piece of wood to make a handle, and he would never trouble them any more. He got it, and then he soon cut them all down. The devil only wants to get the wedge of a little allowed sin into your heart, and you will soon be all his own. It is a wise saying, "There is nothing small between us and God, for God is an infinite God."

There are two ways of coming down from the top of a ladder; one is to jump down, and the other is to come down by the steps: but both will lead you to the bottom. So also there are two ways of going to hell; one is to walk into it with your eyes open--few people do that; the other is to go down by the steps of little sins--and that way, I fear, is only too common. Put up with a few little sins, and you will soon want a few more. Even a heathen could say, "Who was ever content with only one sin?" If you put up with little sins then your path in life will be worse and worse every year. Jeremy Taylor very clearly described the progress of sin in a man:

First it startles him, then it becomes pleasing, then easy, then delightful, then frequent, then habitual, then a way of life! Then the man feels no guilt, then obstinate, then resolves never to repent, and then he is damned.

Young men, if you don't want to come to this, remember the rule I give you this day--resolve at once to break off every known sin.

(2) RESOLVE, BY GOD'S HELP, TO SHUN EVERYTHING WHICH MAY PROVE AN OCCASION OF SIN.

It is an excellent saying, "He that would be safe from the acts of evil, must widely avoid the occasions." There is an old fable, that the butterfly once asked the owl how she should deal with the fire, which had singed her wings; and the owl counseled her, in reply, not to even look at its smoke. It is not enough that we determine not to commit sin, we must carefully keep at a distance from all approaches to it. By this test we ought to examine the ways we spend our time--the books that we read, the friends that we visit, the part of society which we interact with. We must not be content with saying, "There is nothing wrong here;" we must go further, and say, "Is there anything here which may cause me to sin?"

This is one great reason why idleness is to be avoided. It is not that doing nothing is of itself so wicked; it is the opportunity it affords to evil and empty thoughts; it is the wide door it opens for Satan to throw in the seeds of bad things; it is this which is mainly to be feared. If David had not given opportunity to the devil, by walking on his house-top in Jerusalem with nothing to do, he probably never would have seen Bathsheba bathing, nor murdered her husband Uriah.

This, too, is one good reason why worldly entertainments are so objectionable. It may be difficult, in some instances, to show that they are, in themselves, positively unscriptural and wrong. But there is little difficulty in showing that the tendency of almost all of them is most injurious to the soul. They sow the seeds of an earthly and sensual frame of mind. They war against the life of faith. They promote an unhealthy and unnatural craving after excitement. They minister to the lust of the flesh, and the lust of the eye, and the pride of life. They dim the view of heaven and eternity, and give a false color to the things of time. They take away time for private prayer, and Scripture reading, and calm communion with God. The man who mingles in them is like one who gives Satan an advantage. He has a battle to fight, and he gives his enemy the help of sun, and wind, and hill. It would indeed be strange if he did not find himself continually overcome.

Young men, endeavor, as much as you can, to keep clear of everything which may prove injurious to your soul. People may say you are too conscientious, too particular, and ask where is the great harm of such and such things? But don't listen to them. It is dangerous to play tricks with sharp tools: it is far more dangerous to take liberties with your immortal soul. He that would be safe must not come near the brink of danger. He must look on his heart as a barrel of gunpowder, and be cautious not to handle one spark of temptation more than he can help.

What is the use of your praying, "Lord keep me from temptation," unless you are careful not to run into it and "keep me from evil," unless you show a desire to keep out of its way? Take an example from Joseph--Not merely did he refuse solicitation to sin from his master's wife, but he showed his prudence in refusing to even be "with her" (Genesis 39:10). Take to heart the advice of Solomon, not only to "Not set foot on the path of the wicked," but to "Avoid it, do not travel on it; turn from it and go your way" (Proverbs 4:15); "Do not gaze at wine when it is red, when it sparkles in the cup, when it goes down smoothly!" (Proverbs 23:31). The man who took the vow of a Nazarite in Israel, not only took no wine, but be even abstained from grapes in any shape whatever. "Hate what is evil," says Paul to the Romans (Romans 12:9); not merely not to do it; "Flee the evil desires of youth," he writes to Timothy; get away from them as far as possible (2 Timothy 2:22). Oh, how needful are such cautions! Dinah just had go out among the wicked Shechemites, to see their ways, and she lost her virginity. Lot just had pitched his tent near sinful Sodom, and he lost everything but his life.

Young men, be wise with your time. Do not always be trying to see how near you can allow the enemy of souls to come, and yet escape him. Hold him at arm's length. Try to keep clear of temptation as far as possible, and this will be one great help to keep clear of sin.

(3) RESOLVE NEVER TO FORGET THE EYE OF GOD.

The eye of God! Think of that. Everywhere, in every house, in every field, in every room, in every company, alone or in a crowd, the eye of God is always on you. "The eyes of the Lord are everywhere, keeping watch on the wicked and the good" (Proverbs 15:3), and they are eyes that read hearts as well as actions.

Endeavor, I beg you, to realize this fact. Remember that you have to deal with an all-seeing God, a God who never sleeps, a God who understands your thoughts, and with whom the night shines as the day. You may leave your father's house, and go away, like the prodigal, into a far country, and think that there is nobody to watch your conduct; but the eye and ear of God are there before you. You may deceive your parents or employers, you may tell them lies, and act one way before their faces, and another behind their backs, but you cannot deceive God. He knows you through and through. He heard what you said as you came here today. He knows what you are thinking of at this minute. He has set your most secret sins in the light of His countenance, and they will one day come out before the world to your shame, except you take heed.

How little is this really felt! How many things are done continually, which men would never do if they thought they were seen! How many matters are transacted in the rooms of imagination, which would never bear the light of day! Yes; men entertain thoughts in private, and say words in private, and do acts in private, which they would be ashamed and blush to have exposed before the world. The sound of a footstep coming has stopped many a deed of wickedness. A knock at the door has caused many an evil work to be hastily suspended, and hurriedly laid aside. But oh, what miserable folly is all this! There is an all-seeing Witness with us wherever we go. Lock the door, pull down the blind, turn out the light; it doesn't matter, it makes no difference; God is everywhere, you cannot shut Him out, or prevent His seeing. "Nothing in all creation is hidden from God's sight. Everything is uncovered and laid bare before the eyes of him to whom we must give account" (Hebrews 4:13). Young Joseph understood this well when his employer's wife tempted him. There was no one in the house to see them, no human eye to witness against him; but Joseph was one who lived as seeing Him that is invisible: "How could I do such a wicked thing and sin against God?" (Genesis 39:9)

Young men, I ask all of you to read Psalm 139. I advise all of you to learn it by heart. Make it the test of all your dealings in this world's business: say to yourself often, "Do I remember that God sees me?"

Live as in the sight of God. This is what Abraham did, he walked before Him. This is what Enoch did, he walked with Him. This is what heaven itself will be, the eternal presence of God. Do nothing that you would not like God to see. Say nothing, you would not like God to hear. Write nothing, you would not like God to read. Go no place where you would not like God to find you. Read no book of which you would not like God to say, "Show it to Me." Never spend your time in such a way that you would not like to have God say, "What are you doing?"

(4) BE DILIGENT IN THE PRACTICE OF YOUR CHRISTIANITY.

Be regular in going to church, whenever it is open for prayer and preaching, and it is in your power to attend. Be regular in keeping, the Lord's day holy, and determine that God's day out of the seven shall always be given to its rightful owner.

I would not want to leave any false impression on your minds. Do not go away and say I told you that going to church made up the whole of Christianity. I will tell you no such thing. I have no wish to see you grow up formalists and Pharisees. If you think the mere carrying of your body to a certain building, at certain times, on a certain day in the week, will make you a Christian, and prepare you to meet God, I tell you flatly you are miserably deceived. All services without heart-service are unprofitable and vain. They only are true worshipers who "Worship the Father in spirit and in truth, for they are the kind of worshipers the Father seeks" (John 4:23).

But the practices of Christianity are not to be despised because they are not saviors. Gold is not food, you cannot eat it, but you would not say it is useless, and throw it away. Your soul's eternal wellbeing most certainly does not depend on the practices of Christianity, but it is certain that without them, as a general rule, your soul will not do well. God might take all who are saved to heaven in a chariot of fire, as He did Elijah, but He does not do so. He might teach them all by visions, and dreams, and miraculous interventions, without requiring them to read or think for themselves, but He does not do so. And why not? Because He is a God that works by means, and it is His law and will that in all man's dealings with Him means shall be used. No one but a fool would think of building a house without ladders and scaffolding, and just so no wise man will despise means.

I dwell on this point, because Satan will try hard to fill your minds with arguments against the practices of Christianity. He will draw your attention to the numbers of persons who use them and are no better for the using. "See there," he will whisper, "do you not observe that those who go to church are no better than those who stay away?" But do not let this move you. It is never fair to argue against a thing because it is improperly used. It does not follow that the practices of Christianity can do no good because many do them and get no good from them. Medicine is not to be despised because many take it and do not recover their health. No man would think of giving up eating, and drinking because others choose to eat and drink improperly, and so make themselves sick. The value of the practices of Christianity, like other things, depends, in a great measure, on the manner and spirit in which we use them.

I dwell on this point too, because of the strong anxiety I feel that every young man should regularly hear the preaching of Christ's gospel. I cannot tell you how important I think this is. By God's blessing, the ministry of the gospel might be the means of converting your soul, of leading you to a saving knowledge of Christ, of making you a child of God in action and in truth. This would indeed be cause for eternal thankfulness. This would be an event over which angels would rejoice. But even if this were not the case, there is a restraining power and influence in the ministry of the gospel, under which I earnestly desire every young man to be brought. There are thousands whom it keeps back from evil, though it has not yet turned them to God--it has made them far better members of society--though it has not yet made them true Christians. There is a certain kind of mysterious power in the faithful preaching of the gospel, which has an effect on multitudes who listen to it without receiving it into their hearts. To hear sin exposed for what it is, and holiness lifted up, to hear Christ exalted, and the words of the devil denounced--to hear the kingdom of heaven and its blessedness described, and the world and its emptiness exposed; to hear this week after week, Sunday after Sunday, is seldom without a good effect to the soul. It makes it far harder afterwards to run out and commit gross sins. It acts as a wholesome check upon a man's heart. This, I believe, is one way in which that promise of God is made good, "My word that goes out from my mouth: it will not return to me empty" (Isaiah 55:11). There is so much truth in that strong saying of Whitefield, "The gospel keeps many a person from going to jail and from being hanged, if it does not keep him from hell."

Let me name another point which is closely connected with this subject. Let nothing ever tempt you to become a Christian who does not make every effort to attend church on Sunday and make the day special to the Lord. Make up your mind to give all your Sundays to God. A spirit of disregard for this day is growing up among us with fearful rapidity, and not least among young men. Sunday vacations, Sunday visiting, Sunday excursions, to the exclusion of church attendance and honoring of the Lord, are becoming more common every year than they were, and are doing infinite harm to souls.

Young men, be jealous on this point. Whether you live in the city or in the country, take up a decided line; resolve not to miss church on Sunday and the fellowship of God's people. Do not let the plausible argument of "needing to sleep-in to rest your body," do not let not the example of all those around you, do not let the invitation of companions pull you away from fellowship and worship; let none of these things move you to depart from this settled rule, that Sunday's are for God's honor and for fellowship with His people.

Once you don't consider Sundays important or anything special in your Christian life, then in the end you will give up caring for your soul. The steps which lead to this conclusion are easy and common. Begin with not honoring the Lord's Day, and you will soon not honor God's people; cease to honor God's book; and in time you will give God no honor at all. Let a man lay the foundation of having no respect for God's worship or the fellowship of the saints, and I am never surprised if he finishes with no God. It is a remarkable saying of Judge Hale, "Of all the persons who were convicted of capital crimes while he was on the bench, he found only a few who would not confess, on inquiry, that they began their career of wickedness by a neglect of the church and God's people."

Young men, you may have friends who forget the honor of the Lord's day; but resolve, by God's help, that you will always remember to keep it special. Honor it by a regular attendance at some place where the gospel is preached. Settle down under a faithful ministry, and once settled, let your place in church never be empty. Believe me, you will find a special blessing following you: "If you keep your feet from breaking the Sabbath and from doing as you please on my holy day, if you call the Sabbath a delight and the LORD'S holy day honorable, and if you honor it by not going your own way and not doing as you please or speaking idle words, then you will find your joy in the LORD, and I will cause you to ride on the heights of the land and to feast on the inheritance of your father Jacob" (Isaiah 58:13-14). And one thing is very certain, your feelings about Sunday and the fellowship will always be a test and criterion of your fitness for heaven. Fellowship and worship are a foretaste and a fragment of heaven. The man who finds them a burden and not a privilege, may be sure that his heart stands in need of a mighty change.

(5) RESOLVE THAT WHEREVER YOU ARE, YOU WILL PRAY.

Prayer is the life-breath of a man's soul. Without it, we may have a name to live, and be counted Christians; but we are dead in the sight of God. The feeling that we must cry to God for mercy and peace is a mark of salvation; and the habit of spreading before Him our soul's needs is an evidence that we have the spirit of adoption. And prayer is the appointed way to obtain the relief of our spiritual necessities. It opens the treasury, and sets the fountain flowing. If we don't have, it is because we don't ask.

Prayer is the way to procure the outpouring of the Spirit upon our hearts. Jesus has promised the Holy Spirit, the Comforter. He is ready to come down with all His precious gifts, renewing, sanctifying, purifying, strengthening, cheering, encouraging, enlightening, teaching, directing, guiding, into all truth. But then He waits to be asked.

And here it is, I say it with sorrow, here it is that men fall short so miserably. Few indeed are to be found who pray: there are many who go down on their knees, and say a form perhaps, but few who pray; few who cry out to God, few who call on the Lord, few who seek as if they wanted to find, few who knock as if they hungered and thirsted, few who wrestle, few who strive with God earnestly for an answer, few who give Him no rest, few who continue in prayer, few who pray always without ceasing and do not grow weak. Yes: few pray! It is just one of the things assumed as a matter of course, but seldom practiced; a thing which is everybody's business, but in fact hardly anybody performs.

Young men, believe me, if your soul is to be saved, you must pray. God has no speechless children. If you are to resist the world, the flesh, and the devil, you must pray: it is in vain to look for strength in the hour of trial, if it has not been sought for. You may be thrown in with those who never do it, you may have to sleep in the same room with someone who never asks anything of God, still, mark my words, you must pray.

I can believe that you find it difficult to do, difficulties about opportunities to pray, and times to pray, and places to pray. I dare not lay down too strict rules on such points as these. I leave them to your own conscience. You must be guided by circumstances. Our Lord Jesus Christ prayed on a mountain; Isaac prayed in the fields; Hezekiah turned his face to the wall as he lay upon his bed; Daniel prayed by the riverside; Peter, the Apostle, on the housetop. I have heard of young men praying in stables and haylofts. All that I contend for is this, you must know what it is to "go into your room, close the door and pray to your Father, who is unseen" (Matthew 6:6). There must be stated times when you must speak to God face to face, you must every day have your times for prayer--You must pray.

Without this, all my advice and counsel is useless. This is that piece of spiritual armor which Paul names last in his list, in Ephesians 6, but it is in truth that is first in value and importance. This is that meat which you must eat daily, if you would travel safely through the wilderness of this life. It is only in the strength of this that you will get onward towards the mountain of God. I have heard it said that some people who grind metal sometimes wear a magnetic mouthpiece at their work, which catches all the fine metal dust that flies around them, prevents it from entering their lungs, and so saves their lives. Prayer is the mouthpiece that you must wear continually, or else you will never work uninjured by the unhealthy atmosphere of this sinful world. You must pray.

Young men, be sure no time is so well spent as that which a man spends on his knees. Make time for this, whatever your situation may be. Think of David, King of Israel: what does be say? "Evening, morning and noon I cry out in distress, and he hears my voice" (Psalm 55:17). Think of Daniel. He had all the business of a kingdom on his hands; yet he prayed three times a day. See there the secret of his safety in wicked Babylon. Think of Solomon. He begins his reign with prayer for help and assistance, and hence his wonderful prosperity. Think of Nehemiah. He could find time to pray to the God of heaven, even when standing in the presence of his master, Artaxerxes. Think of the example these good men have left you, and go and do likewise.

Oh that the Lord may give you all the spirit of grace and supplication! "Have you not just called to me: 'My Father, my friend from my youth'" (Jeremiah 3:4). Gladly would I consent to the fact that all of this message should be forgotten, if only this doctrine of the importance of prayer might be impressed on your hearts.

V. CONCLUSION

And now I hurry towards a conclusion. I have said things that many perhaps will not like, and not receive; but I appeal to your consciences, Are they not true?

Young men, you all have consciences. Corrupt and ruined by the fall as we are, each of us has a conscience. In a corner of each heart there sits a witness for God, a witness who condemns when we do wrong, and approves when we do right. To that witness I make my appeal this day, are not the things that I have been saying true?

Go then, young men, and resolve this day to remember your Creator in the days of your youth. Before the day of grace is past, before your conscience has become hardened by age, and deadened by repeated trampling under foot, while you have strength, and time, and opportunities, go and join yourself to the Lord in an everlasting covenant not to be forgotten. The Spirit will not always strive. The voice of conscience will become feebler and fainter every year you continue to resist it. The Athenians said to Paul, "We want to hear you again on this subject" but they had heard him for the last time (Acts 17:32). Make haste, and don't delay. Linger and hesitate no more.

Think of the unspeakable comfort you will give to parents, relatives, and friends, if you take my counsel. They have expended time, money, and health to raise you, and make you what you are. Surely they deserve some consideration. Who can know the joy and gladness which young people have in their power to give? Who can tell the anxiety and sorrow that sons like Esau, and Hophni, and Phinehas, and Absalom may cause? Truly indeed does Solomon say, "A wise son brings joy to his father, but a foolish son grief to his mother" (Proverbs 10:1). Oh, consider these things, and give God your heart! Let it not be said of you at last, as it is of many, that your "youth was a disorder, your manhood a struggle, and your old age a regret."

Think of the good you might be doing for the world. Almost all the eminent saints of God sought the Lord early. Moses, Samuel, David, Daniel, all served God from their youth. God seems to delight in putting special honor upon young servants; and think of what we could expect, if young men in our own day would consecrate the springtime of their lives to God? Workers are wanted now in almost every great and good cause, and cannot be found. Technology of every kind for spreading truth exists, but there are not people to make it work.

Money is more easily obtained for doing good than men. Ministers are wanted for new churches, missionaries are wanted for new fields, teachers are wanted for Sunday School, many a good cause is standing still merely for want of workers. The supply of godly, faithful, trustworthy men, for posts like those I have named, is far below the demand.

Young men of the present day, you are wanted for God. This is an age of activity. We are shaking off some of our past selfishness. Men no longer sleep the sleep of apathy and indifference about others, as their forefathers did. They are beginning to be ashamed of thinking like Cain, "Am I my brother's keeper?" A wide field of usefulness is open before you, if you are only willing to enter into it. The harvest is great, and the workers are few. Be zealous of good works. Come, come to the aid of the Lord against the wickedness of this age.

This is, in some sort, to be like God, not only good, but doing good (Psalm 119:68). This is the way to follow the steps of your Lord and Savior: "He went around doing good" (Acts 10:38).

And who can doubt that this is the path which makes an immortal soul beautiful? Who would not rather leave this world like Josiah, grieved by all, than depart like Jehoram, "to no one's regret?" (2 Chronicles 21:20). Is it better to be idle, frivolous, to live for your body, your selfishness, your lusts, and your pride, or to spend and be spent in the glorious cause of usefulness to your fellow men--to be a blessing to your country and the world, to be the friend of the prisoner and the captive, to be the spiritual father of hundreds of immortal souls in heathen lands, to be a burning and a shining light, an epistle of Christ, known and read of all men, the inspiration of every Christian heart that comes across your path? Oh, who can doubt? Who can for one moment doubt?

Young men, consider your responsibilities. Think of the privilege and luxury of doing good. Resolve this day to be useful. Give your hearts at once to Christ.

Think, lastly, of the happiness that will come to your own soul, if you serve God, happiness as you travel through life, and happiness in the end, when the journey is over. Believe me, whatever vain notions you may have heard, believe me, there is a reward for the righteous even in this world. Godliness has indeed the promise of this life, as well as of that which is to come. There is a solid peace in feeling that God is your friend. There is a real satisfaction in knowing that however your unworthiness, you are complete in Christ, that you have an enduring portion, that you have chosen that good part which shall not be taken from you.

The backslider in heart may well be content with his own ways, but "the good man [will be] rewarded for his" (Proverbs 14:14). The path of the worldly man grows darker and darker every year that he lives; the path of the Christian is like a shining light, brighter and brighter to the very end. His sun is just rising when the sun of the worldly is setting forever; his best things are all beginning to blossom and bloom forever, when those of the worldly are all slipping out of his hands, and passing away.

Young men, these things are true. Listen to the word of exhortation. Be persuaded. Take up the cross. Follow Christ. Yield yourselves to God.

Made in the USA
Columbia, SC
03 June 2023